Listening and Talking:
A Guide to
Promoting Spoken Language
in Young Hearing-Impaired Children

Listening and Talking:
A Guide to Promoting Spoken Language in Young Hearing-Impaired Children

Elizabeth B. Cole, Ed.D.
McGill University
Montreal, Quebec

With a Contribution by
Drs. Richard and Laura Kretschmer
University of Cincinnati
Cincinnati, Ohio

Alexander Graham Bell Association for the Deaf
3417 Volta Place, N.W. Washington, D.C. 20007

Library of Congress Cataloging in Publication Data

Cole, Elizabeth B., *Listening and Talking: A Guide to Promoting Spoken Language in Young Hearing-impaired Children*

Cover Art: Peter Roper/William Marler

Card Catalog Number 91-076740
ISBN 0-88200-172-8
© 1992 Alexander Graham Bell
Association for the Deaf
3417 Volta Place, N.W.
Washington, D.C. 20007

Printed in the United States of America
10 9 8 7 6 5 4 3 2 1

Dedication

To Pat Hackworth and **Tina Prewarski** . . . . both of whom got me hooked on it all, those many short years ago.

and

To Richard and **Laura Kretschmer** and **Daniel Ling**
. . . . all of whom I have been so fortunate to have known as esteemed teachers, mentors, colleagues, and treasured friends.

Contents

(All sections on "Communication and Language Developments" in Chapter 4 are contributed by Richard and Laura Kretschmer.)

Acknowledgments

Many authors, in listing the colleagues and friends who helped them in significant ways, feel compelled to issue a disclaimer assuring the reader that those people should share only in the praise the book receives, not in any of the responsibility for its deficiencies. That is clearly fallacious. If the acknowledgees contributed to making the book as good as the author feels it is, then surely an even greater effort on their part would have made it even better. . . . I am grateful to the . . . individuals who must share the blame with me.
(Kenneth Kaye, 1982, p. ix)

I would like to begin by acknowledging all those whose ideas have "wormed their way into this work in devious ways" (Kaye, 1982, p. ix). This would have to include Richard and Laura Kretschmer and Daniel Ling at the very top of the list. Their ideas about language, speech, and audition have irreparably shaped this book. Others who must be held accountable for valuable contributions include (in alphabetical order) Arlie Adam, Martha Crago, Ciwa Griffiths, Lisa Handsley, Grace Harris, Harold Johnson, Doris Leckie, Muriel Mischook, Winifred Northcott, Marietta Paterson, Nan Phillips, Doreen Pollack, Audrey Simmons-Martin, Judy Simser, Jacqueline St. Clair-Stokes, and Pat Stone.

Next I disclaim responsibility for any flaws in the cogency or clarity of the book that many hours of dedicated and talented editing and "word-smithing" by Daniel Ling and Robert Leckie did not uncover and resolve.

And last, there are three people who must share the blame for helping me to maintain a modicum of sanity, perspective, and good humor during what have been several challenging book-writing years: the precious center of my own interactional life—Frank, Thea, and Ted Zimnicki.

About the Author

Elizabeth Cole with daughter, Thea and son, Ted.

Dr. Elizabeth Cole is an associate professor of Aural Habilitation at McGill University, Montreal. Her teaching and research center around parent-infant interaction, the use of residual hearing, and the development of spoken language in young hearing-impaired children. Born in Freeport, Illinois, she was a French teacher in New Hampshire, an American Peace Corps TOESL teacher/instructor in India, and a teacher of reading and study skills to pre-med students in Kentucky prior to coming to the field of hearing-impairment. Dr. Cole had all of these speech and language-related activities to draw upon when she began doing parent guidance and teaching young hearing-impaired children at the (then) Lexington Deaf Oral School in Kentucky, in 1973. She received her M.S. in Audiology and her Ph.D. in Special Education (Hearing-Impairment) at the University of Cincinnati before accepting a faculty position at McGill University in 1980. At McGill, she later became Director of both the graduate training program in Auditory-Oral Habilitation and Education of the Hearing-Impaired, and the McGill University Project for Hearing-Impaired Children, (a parent-infant guidance program).

Since becoming a professor, Dr. Cole has lectured on speech and spoken language intervention in Canada, the United States, England, and Australia, and has contributed numerous articles to the professional literature on hearing impairment. Dr. Cole is a certified member (audiology) of the American-Speech-Language-Hearing Association

(ASHA) and of the Canadian Association of Speech-Language Pathologists and Audiologists (CASLPA), has served on the Board of Directors of the Association of College Educators of the Hearing-Impaired, the Board of Directors at the Montreal Oral School for the Deaf, and is president-elect of the International Organization of Educators of the Hearing-Impaired, the professional section of the Alexander Graham Bell Association for the Deaf. Her husband Frank, five-year-old Thea, and fifteen-month-old Ted continuously teach her about spoken language development and parent-child interaction.

Introduction

Acquisition of any language system is never an end in itself, but rather a means to induct children into full human experiences.
(Streng, Kretschmer, and Kretschmer, 1978, p. 69)

The goal of this text is to provide a framework for professionals who want to help parents promote spoken language development in their very young hearing-impaired children. Ideas in the text are grounded on three basic assumptions. The first assumption is that it makes sense to help the **parent** help the child, because this is the manner in which the most effective intervention with very young children is achieved (Bromwich, 1981; Bronfenbrenner, 1974; Garland, Swanson, Stoner, and Woodruff, 1981). The second is that it makes sense to begin intervention with the **very young** hearing-impaired children (birth-to-three years old) because of the verbal and academic deficits often seen in children whose audiologic and educational management begin later (Geers and Moog, 1989; Smith and Strain, 1988). The third is that it makes sense to help these children learn to **talk** in order to keep as much as possible of the world open and available to them. The full human experience referred to in the Streng, Kretschmer, and Kretschmer quotation includes development of a self-concept, formation of interpersonal relationships, and acquisition of knowledge and understanding of the world. Language ability can make a difference for learning in each of these areas.

The reader will note that a number of ideas in this book could apply to learning sign language as well as to learning spoken language. However, the intended focus here is on spoken language develop-

1

ment. This is not to imply that a single "method" or collection of methods can meet the needs of all hearing-impaired children. It is, rather, an attempt to provide an in-depth examination of how to develop one vitally important component of the needs of the vast majority of hearing-impaired children in the full range of "oral" and "total communication" programs. The advantages of fluent spoken language abilities are self-evident for academic achievement, as well as for social and economic well-being in the "mainstream" hearing world (e.g. *ASHA*, 1979; Pflaster, 1980, 1981). With recent technologic advances in early audiological diagnostic techniques and in hearing instruments, this goal of fluent spoken language can be realized for more and more hearing-impaired children, including the majority of those with hearing losses described as "profound."[1]

Not every severely or profoundly hearing-impaired child does learn to talk, sometimes in spite of the best efforts of parents and professionals. Reasons for a lack of satisfactory progress in spoken language can include late diagnosis, poorly fitting and/or poorly maintained hearing aids, an impoverished educational program, lack of appropriate sensory aids for those with no measurable hearing, insufficient or ineffective parental involvement, additional handicaps, and problems in learning which are either general or specific in nature. None of these factors by themselves preclude the possibility of the child learning to talk, but a combination of several of them can mitigate against it. Fortunately, however, these reasons either do not or need not apply for most hearing-impaired children.

Today the Alexander Graham Bell Association for the Deaf lists approximately one hundred and fifty programs in North America, both publicly and privately supported, that provide "auditory-oral" services for hearing-impaired children in the birth- to three-year-old age range. Naturally, there are an unspecified additional number of programs which do not happen to be listed with the Alexander Graham Bell Association. While the primary aim of all of these early intervention programs is to help the children learn to talk, close inspection reveals that such programs vary on several theoretical and methodological dimensions.

---

[1]The conventional "profound" hearing loss is any pure tone average loss of 91 dB or greater (Davis, 1970; Yantis, 1985).

1. **The nature and manner of parent involvement in the child's learning can be different in different programs.** This can be reflected in details such as the number of sessions per week; whether or not the parent is in the therapy room or observing from outside; whether it is primarily the parent or the therapist who interacts with the child during the sessions; the locale of the sessions (center-based versus home-based); the existence of parent group presentations and activities outside of the sessions; and the nature and amount of information supplied to the parent.

2. **Programs vary in the emphasis placed on normal everyday interactive events as the context within which the child will learn language versus an emphasis on adult-directed teaching activities.** A program's perspective on this issue can be reflected in whether or not the parent is expected to go home and engage in activities such as teaching particular speech sounds, vocabulary, or sentence patterns, or attempting to replicate the therapy sessions's activities. The balance between these everyday interactive events and adult-directed teaching activities may vary within a program depending upon the child's age and degree of hearing loss. That is, the older and "deafer" the child, the more likely it is that he will receive more structured, adult-directed instruction.

3. **The use of sense modalities in providing language input, both in normal everyday conversations and in more adult-directed activities is another dimension that varies widely among programs and interventionists.** There are three possible avenues of sensory input for spoken language: auditory, visual, and tactile:

    a. The *auditory* sense modality can be maximized in normal conversation (for example) by speaking at a relatively close distance to the child, by sitting behind or beside him, by obscuring the child's view of the lips using the hand or a piece of paper, or by having the child's visual focus on the toys or activity at hand, rather than on the speaker's lips. In the teaching of specific speech sounds, for example, the salient acoustic characteristics of particular phonemes can be highlighted by presenting them with certain other phonemes, or by presenting them in particular syllabic positions. Clearly, reliance on the auditory sense modality demands a commitment to rigorous audiological assessment and monitoring.

Cochlear implants merit special mention in this context of input-providing devices for hearing-impaired children. They are considered by Rosen, Walliker, Brimacombe, and Edgerton (1989) to provide "electro-auditory" stimulation. Their full potential is only beginning to be tapped as data accumulate on the first very young profoundly deaf children who are learning spoken language using either single or multiple electrode cochlear implants.

b. The *visual* sense modality in this context refers to whether or not the child has access to the cues provided by speech-reading—that is, for example, through watching the speaker's lips and facial expressions. Further, although it is now only rarely done with young children, it is also possible to consciously teach differentiations among or between particular lip positions and their associated sounds (e.g. the difference in lip position and movement of a /fa/ versus a /ba/).

c. The *tactile* sense modality can be employed in a global way though the use of vibrotactile devices that are intended to be worn by the child to aid in perception of speech in normal conversational situations. Vibrotactile devices are also sometimes used in a more limited way for speech and auditory training exercises. With or without a vibrotactile aid, touch can be employed in demonstrating features of particular speech sounds where tactile sensation is salient such as the breath stream of fricatives and plosives.

Some of the possible permutations of the use of sense modalities include programs that advocate the use of audition only; programs that advocate the use of audition first and whenever possible, but include the use of vision and touch as supplements when needed; programs that always allow the child to watch the face when someone is speaking (and are thus presenting the input through audition and vision), and use touch also, as needed; programs where the children wear a vibrotactile device or cochlear implant as well as their hearing aid(s) and thus are receiving tactile or electro-auditory, auditory, and visual input; and programs which might do any of the above, depending upon the needs and abilities of a particular child.

To the uninitiated, these differences may seem to be insignificant, but within the field of education of the hearing-impaired, they have, with some justification, been hotly contested issues. In view of this discord, both professionals and parents may be able to find some measure of reassurance in the fact that oral programs and teachers espousing the full variety of combinations of these dimensions have **all** been producing hearing-impaired children who learn to talk. The key elements seem to rest most squarely on the knowledge, persistence, and enthusiasm of the teacher and the parents as they do whatever they do. This text is intended to provide some of that knowledge, while the persistence and enthusiasm will need to come from somewhere else.

A great deal has already been written about how to help hearing-impaired children learn to talk. The present work is not intended to provide comprehensive coverage of all aspects of intervention for very young hearing-impaired children. Rather, the intention is to fill in some missing pieces about helping parents to help their children develop intelligible spoken language, and to integrate already existing knowledge in a unique and scholarly manner.

Chapter 1 provides background information about spoken language, about theories of language learning, and about related organizational principles for intervention with hearing-impaired children. Chapter 2 describes the normal language-learning scene in some detail. Following discussion of the child's early learning of the rudiments of communication, the chapter concentrates on the vitally important characteristics of the caregiver's talk as he or she interacts with the infant or young child. Chapters 1 and 2 set a research-based backdrop for Chapter 3 where the research on interactions between caregivers and hearing-impaired children is considered, and guidelines for analyzing caregiver interactional behaviors are provided.

Chapter 4 outlines clusters of child achievements which occur as language is acquired. The intention is to provide a current, research-based guide for roughly sequential expectations for the child's language-learning. That is, it is a guide to what can be considered "fair game" for highlighting in the course of everyday events, for planning intervention activities, as well as for assessment and descriptive documentation of progress.

Chapter 5 considers auditory abilities which should be developing along with the spoken language abilities. These auditory abilities receive separate mention, lest anyone believe that simply putting on hearing aids and interacting normally with a hearing-impaired child will automatically result in his or her learning to talk. That **may** actually work for children with mild-to-moderate degrees of hearing loss. But for many others, who are severely or profoundly hearing-impaired, it is likely to be inadequate. The adults in such children's lives usually need to internalize strategies for stimulating and promoting auditory and motor speech abilities not only though normal everyday events, but through specific embellishments of those everyday events.

Chapter 6 integrates all of the preceding chapters, in detailing the implementation of intervention with parents and their hearing-impaired infants. It discusses both the affect and content agendas of intervention, and provides practical guidelines and strategies.

As mentioned above, this book is not intended to cover every area of importance for professionals to carry out intervention with hearing-impaired infants and their parents. One crucially important area which was purposely omitted is that of the audiologic management of the child. In the last fifteen years, tremendous technologic advances have been made in infant hearing assessment capabilities, hearing instruments, cochlear implants, and vibrotactile devices; earmold coupling systems; and devices for quickly and accurately monitoring the function and benefit of the hearing aids, as well as the status of the child's middle ear. These permit a degree of precision in evaluating and monitoring which means that rigorous audiological management of hearing-impaired children is well within reach. This vitally important area merits its own in-depth treatment in other sources. Indeed, the integration of technology into the educational management of hearing-impaired children has been the subject of a recent text by Ling (1989). Interventionists must make every effort to be fully informed and up-to-date in this area, which continues to change at a very rapid rate.

Spoken Language and Intervention

Language is what language does.
(Anonymous)

Since this book is so centrally concerned with spoken language-learning by young children, it is appropriate to begin the first chapter with a discussion of all that is involved in communicating verbally, and of how much of that learning is accomplished at a very young age. Theories about how children learn to talk are addressed next, followed by consideration of the relevance of the nature/nurture controversy for intervention. The final section in this chapter concerns the overall organization of spoken language intervention for hearing-impaired children based on current informed views of the effects of hearing loss on psychological and cognitive processing.

What's Involved In "Talking"?

A recently popularized term in the language-learning literature is "communicative competence," a term originally borrowed from Hymes

(1971). He describes communicative competence as including how to say something, what to say, when to say it, where to say it, and to whom to say it. Hymes' seminal thinking is frequently referenced in the "pragmatics" literature explosion which began in the mid-1970's. What was new in Hymes' conception was the importance of the appropriate **use** of language. Communicative competence thus includes knowledge about the cultural, interpersonal, and linguistic appropriateness of talk in particular contexts (Rice, 1986). Roth and Spekman (1984) have delineated three interwoven domains of communicative knowledge which the child eventually acquires, thus enabling him to use language appropriately.

One of these levels of pragmatic knowledge is presuppositional knowledge that governs the automatic choice of an appropriate register for expressing oneself in a particular social context. The child must learn that it is important to attend to and interpret particular features of the listener (e.g. age, sex, social, and educational status) and the setting in order to determine the degree of informativeness and politeness which is appropriate to a particular situation. This information contributes to the types of sentence structures used, the directness or indirectness of reference, and a host of other grammatical choices such as how much to use pronouns, subordinate clauses, and adjective embeddings.

Presuppositional knowledge also influences the decisions regarding the level of explicitness taken in Roth and Spekman's second pragmatic domain: the functions or intentions expressed by each utterance. The infant initially uses his gestures and words to demand, ask, and label things (Dore, 1978). By age three, that number of functions is expanded by at least ten-fold to include expression of subtle intentions such as suggestions and hints rather than direct demands (Dore, Gearhart, and Newman, 1978).

The third of these interrelated domains of communicative knowledge concerns the conventions regarding the social organization of discourse—or the mostly unspoken rules for maintaining a dialogue with another person. These include conventional turn-taking, topic initiation and maintenance, and repair procedures to follow when there is a breakdown in the communication.

In addition to pragmatics, other rule systems involved in learning to talk are the semantic, syntactic, morphologic, and phonologic systems.

Semantics refers to knowledge of networks or hierarchies of meaning for individual vocabulary words (i.e. lexicon), as well as knowledge of meaning relationships of words in sentences (i.e. case grammar). The syntactic rule system is concerned with the permissible ways of ordering words within sentences in order to express particular meanings, and with ways of transforming basic sentences into more complex structures. Morphologic rules are concerned with the permissible combinations of free morphemes with affixes (such as "un" in "unhappy" or "ness" in "happiness"), and with inflectional morphemes which indicate grammatical features such as tense (The dog walk*ed*.), person (The dog walk*s*.), or number (The dog*s* walk.). The phonological system includes all of the sounds in the language, the permissible ways of combining those sounds into words, and the conventional ways in which the language uses prosodic features such as intonation, stress, and rhythm to express meaning.

Clearly, the learning of all the conventions for pragmatics, semantics, syntax, morphology, and phonology is no small task. The wonder is that by the age of three, most normally developing children have sophisticated knowledge in all of those areas—and that the language development of many school-age, hearing-impaired children, given appropriate auditory and linguistic experience, can be remarkably similar to that of their age peers (e.g. Geers and Moog, 1989; Ling and Milne, 1981).

How Does a Child Learn to Talk?

The fact is that we do not really know just how and/or why language develops (Rice, 1986). Even though "development" implies change, present developmental research and theories seem to be best at describing what goes on within the "plateaus of non-change" (Snow and Gilbreath, 1983). What is not known is how or why the child moves from one kind of knowing or one developmental stage to the next. This is not unlike the situation in other areas of human development, where the motivation or the mechanisms for the transitions from stage to stage are still basically unexplained through research findings (e.g. Emde and Harmon, 1984).

Theoretical explanations of language development have traditionally fallen into either "nature" or "nurture" categories at opposite ends of a continuum. The debate has centered around whether the language acquisition process can be accounted for by innate, internally generated processes [a view usually attributed to nativists such as Chomsky (1966), Gardner (1983), or McNeill (1966)] or by learning, through externally controlled events [the perspective of behaviorists such as Skinner (1957) or Staats (1971)]. Current thinking is that this nature/nurture dichotomy is an artificial bipolarization which has outlived its value.

A third approach, an "interactionist" perspective, seems to hold more explanatory promise. (This is not to be confused with caregiver-child interaction!) There are several varieties of this perspective (See Bohannan and Warren-Leubecker, 1985, for a review), but they all share a recognition and acceptance that both innate and environmental factors determine development. The fundamental idea is that innate, internal, developmental abilities or propensities (some of which may or may not be specifically linguistic) interact with environmental factors and experiences in ultimately building up the child's knowledge of language (Bates and MacWhinney, 1979; Bohannan and Warren-Leubecker, 1985; Cromer, 1981). Examples of the internal factors would include processing biases such as selective auditory and visual attention and processing, categorical perception, and a propensity for attempting to search for order and/or causality in events (Newport, Gleitman, and Gleitman, 1977). The environmental factors would include potentially all of the stable and changing features of the child's social, physical, linguistic, experiential environment; that is, the people and objects around the child throughout his everyday life. Thus, the child's natural, genetic endowment is seen as interacting with his/her social context in determining and promoting the acquisition of linguistic behaviors. With regard to the nature/nurture controversy, Bloom (1983) observes that neither nature nor nurture alone is sufficient to result in language acquisition. She says that the question is no longer "Which one?," but "How?" That is, **how** do biological and environmental factors interact throughout the acquisition process?

Consider for a moment the fascinating time when the child first begins to use words to communicate. In order to support the appearance of those first words, a number of hitherto apparently separate threads of development must converge. The Bloom (1983), Bloom and Lahey (1978), and Lahey (1988) division of language development into **form**, **content**, and **use** components is a useful construct for this brief discussion. "Form" development during the first twelve months of life includes multiple and dramatic changes occurring in the child's vocalizations as they gradually become more and more speech-like (Oller, 1980; Stark, 1980) "Content" development includes the child's gradual acquisition of differentiated repertoires of behaviors for using, pursuing, and/or dealing with objects and with people (Sugarman, 1984). Early "use" development includes the child's integration into the basic back-and-forth rhythm of human interaction (turn-taking), of being responsive and having others respond to him. Bloom (1983) suggests that the transition to the use of words comes about when these separate threads of development begin to intersect. That is, by about twelve months of age, the child knows how to behave interactively with others, his vocal productions are speech-like, and he knows (for example) that a person can be used to get a hard-to-reach toy. Words will appear when all of these types of knowing begin to converge. Clearly, this is a simplistic overview of an extremely complex and multifaceted set of developments. However, there does seem to be intuitive validity to Bloom's concept of developmental transitions occurring when separately developing threads of abilities begin to converge.

To return to the nature/nurture issue, the foregoing discussion is an excellent example of the fact that we can describe what is acquired as the child develops, but we cannot account for why the changes in ability or behavior occurs. Bloom's (1983) view is that the transitions to new levels of functioning require insight or intuitive understanding on the part of the child. Insight and intuitive understanding are unarguably internal to the child, as would be the child's propensity to even begin searching for understanding of the objects and people around him. But these innate abilities would have little value without the environment providing the objects upon which to act or the people with whom to interact. Both nature and nurture seem to be inextricably implicated as mediators in the acquisition of language.

Relevance for Intervention Decisions

Actually, for the educator or therapist with children and families needing immediate attention, the nature/nurture debate may be an interesting but immaterial one. With regard to the nature of the child, some aspects of the child's presenting repertoire undoubtedly are genetically endowed and/or internally generated. This may include aspects such as information processing rate, learning style (e.g. analytic, holistic or some combination thereof), temperament, and the child's facility with language-learning strategies such as the elicitation, entry, and expansion operations proposed by Shatz (1987). The child's genetic endowment clearly cannot be ignored. But for the interventionist, ethical practice demands that all of the child's abilities and inabilities must be considered to be amenable to influence or teaching until demonstrated otherwise.

With regard to the nurturing of the child, there is merit in the notion that language learning is a highly buffered or protected process, and that "the environment needs only to be sufficiently rich that the learner can at any point in time discover what [he] needs. . . ." (Shatz, 1987, p. 4). At least, this may be so for normally developing and normally hearing children. But for children with language-learning problems, there is evidence that differences in the environment can have considerable impact on the child's language development. And even for normally developing children, the defining characteristics of the "sufficiently rich" environment for language learning have yet to be unequivocally articulated. In any case, interventionists think in terms of attempting to determine the components of an *optimally* rich environment, rather than a *sufficiently* rich one. The environment, even with all of its individual and cultural variability, remains an extremely likely candidate for profitable examination and guidance toward becoming as language-facilitating as present scientific knowledge permits.

How Should Intervention Be Organized?

The question that then arises for the interventionist is one of how to organize all of the kinds of learning and knowledge in order to assess the hearing-impaired child's status, and then implement a program intended to guide and promote the child's progress. In order to answer that question, one needs to consider two contrasting views regarding the effects of deafness on psychological and cognitive processing. Studies that have set out to define the effects of deafness on psychological and cognitive processing tend to be unavoidably fraught with weaknesses in experimental design. Sources of experimental weakness include the relatively low incidence of congenital sensori-neural deafness which results in a small subject pool, complicated by the myriad of factors relating to individual differences that can affect the individual's use of residual hearing and learning of language. Research planning is often further limited by ethical questions regarding the withholding of habilitative treatment in order to establish control groups. The result is that for nearly every observation or research finding in this field, there is a counter-finding. Consequently one is left with points of view, and many questions still open to research endeavor.

The traditional view is that, due to the hearing loss, the child's psychological and cognitive processing abilities and strategies are somehow different, or reorganized. The result of this reorganization is language usage and understanding that are different from those of people with normal hearing (Furth, 1966; Myklebust, 1960). Proponents of this view tend to base their arguments on observations of deaf people whose primary mode of communication is sign language. It seems quite logical that one's language usage and understanding would require a different sort of cognitive processing for a language whose semantic and grammatical subtleties are encoded visually, rather than acoustically. But these differences would seem to be more related to the modality or base (visual versus acoustic) through which the language is learned and used—rather than due to the sensori-neural damage in the child's cochlea. In any case, espousing the view of cognitive and psychological difference resulting from deafness might logically lead one to the (circular) belief that visually based language is the "natural" language of the deaf.

A diametrically opposed view, held by the writer and others, is that if adequate auditory and linguistic experience is provided to most hearing-impaired children, then cognitive functioning and organization can be expected to follow the normal course of development (Cole and Gregory, 1986; Kretschmer and Kretschmer, 1978; Ling, 1976, 1989; Ling and Milne, 1981; Streng et al., 1978). Differences in the child's language ability are seen as due to lack of experience and exposure: as delay, rather than as deviance. The sequence of language learning is expected to include normal processes such as the intertwining and interdependency of linguistic and cognitive activity. That is, assuming early and appropriate auditory, communicative, and linguistic stimulation, the hearing-impaired child's early talking is likely to mirror that of his/her hearing peers. For example, early semantic/syntactic performance will focus on objects and people in the immediate environment; the presence, recurrence, and/or disappearance of objects; actions related to the child; possession; basic characteristics of objects; locations in space; and cause and effect (Bloom, 1973; Nelson, 1973). The child is also likely to exhibit normal "errors" such as overgeneralizing or over-restricting syntactic and semantic rules during the learning process (Kretschmer and Kretschmer, 1978).

Assuming that audiological management is rigorous and appropriate, then providing enriched verbal interaction becomes the most important priority in order to promote the child's linguistic and cognitive development. The most reasonable course to follow in carrying out intervention for hearing-impaired children is thus one of replicating (or re-establishing) the overall framework of a normal language-learning environment. The child is expected to develop normal psychological and cognitive function and to follow the usual developmental sequences. However, the provision of adequate auditory and linguistic stimulation requires **embellishments** of the normal situation which undeniably result in it being "non-normal" to some degree. One such embellishment would be the presence of the child's hearing aids and/or FM apparatus. Other embellishments would include the parent consciously employing specific techniques for helping the child learn to use his residual hearing, such as sitting close by (either behind or beside) the child when speaking to him, and using an interesting and animated voice when speaking. Another necessary embellishment would be to increase the frequency of caregiver-child interacting events throughout the day, specifically as an attempt to remedy the child's decreased exposure to spoken language. That is, the hearing-impaired child is likely to have a lessened ability to profit from each instance of interaction, as well as a lessened (or nonexistent) ability to overhear others' interactions with each other (Ling, 1981). Consequently, in order to achieve a desirable level of support, it may be necessary to establish an environment where interacting occurs more consistently and frequently than it normally might (Snow, 1984a). The overall thrust of the parents and of the intervention program is to acknowledge and cope with the differences related to the hearing loss, while attempting to put them into perspective in a scene where most other aspects of interacting with their child will be normal.

2

The Early Language-
Learning Scene

. . . conversation and interactive skills ("communicative competence") are not additional domains in which the child must gain skills, after mastering linguistic form and meaning. Rather, communicative skill, defined dyadically as experience with effective communication, is the source of knowledge about form and meaning. A child who could not already interact could never learn to communicate; a child who cannot communicate would never learn language.
(Snow, 1984b, p. v)

This book focuses on the communication and spoken language developments which occur for normally hearing children between birth and three years of age. This period begins with a time where the child is not actually using words—the time often referred to as "prelinguistic." It continues through a time where the child is interacting in a broad variety of conversational contexts with different people, frequently using grammatically correct, mostly intelligible, four- to six-word utterances. Communication and language-learning achievements of this period are detailed in Chapter 4 in terms of specific pragmatic, semantic, syntactic, morphologic, and phonologic acquisitions, and in Chapter 5 in terms of auditory learning. The present discussion concerns the normal (presumably language-facilitating) interactive environment whose basic features remain important throughout the birth- to three-year-old period. This provides the theoretical background and rationale for the Checklist for Caregivers in Chapter 3, pp. 48–51. Let us begin by considering what happens when a parent and a three-year-old have a conversational exchange.

It is now generally agreed that language develops in the course of interactions between parent and child during routine, everyday play and caregiving activities. The essence of fluent communication between the parent and child consists of sending and receiving linguistically encoded messages. By the time the child is about three years of age, the caregiver or child can seek out the other in order to enjoy, share, request, assist, inform, and/or learn about the world (Dore, 1975; Dore et al., 1978; Halliday, 1975). In order for any communicative attempt by either interactant to be successfully received, there are two necessary conditions: first, a shared focus must be established; and second, the message must be relevant to and interpretable by the listener (Bruner, 1975; Grice, 1967). That is, the parent and child need to be jointly engaged in some activity or looking at each other or an object. And the comment or question that is made needs to be of interest to the listener, as well as understandable. When the initiating attempt is successful, the receiver and sender quickly exchange roles, and a linked communicative chain ensues: the two are thus engaged in a "communicative interaction." The communicative aspect relates to the cycle of shared understanding (messages) sent and received and sent and received. The interactive aspect refers partly to the back-and-forth nature of the event (the taking of turns in a conversation), and partly to the fact that each partner actively derives meaning about the message from details of the participation of the other in the event.

But how do the parent and child arrive at this felicitous level of fluent conversation and interacting? This discussion of the development of communicative interacting will address three related areas: the affective relationship between parent and child, the child's development of interactional abilities; and features of caregiver talk which may be facilitative of the child's development.

The Affective Relationship

Recent literature supports the notion that the affective relationship between parent and child has fundamental importance for the child's acquisition of language from the very beginning. Thoman (1981), for example, sees the child's earliest communication experiences as primarily organized by and around affect. "Affective forms of communication precede, influence, and subsequently become integrated with linguistic (i.e. cognitive) communication . . ." (p. 183). Similarly, Dore (1986) sees language as "emerging out of the mother-infant dialog of affect" (p. 17), so the emotional atmosphere between mother and child may have crucial importance for language-learning.

The question then arises regarding the nature of the affective relationship which would be most supportive of language-learning. It was not the intent of either Dore or Thoman to prescribe the kind of affect which is necessary (or even desirable) for optimal early language development. But it is interesting to note the adjectives scattered throughout Dore's scholarly discussion of "personhood" and the interpersonal motivation for learning language. The environment provided by the parent during at least the early interactions is variously referred to as loving, rational, caring, thoughtful, caressing, joyous (Dore, 1986, pp. 16–18). This nurturant environment is not unlike the environment Clarke-Stewart (1973) found to be most facilitative throughout infancy for social-emotional, intellectual, and linguistic development: ". . . not only warm, loving, and nonrejecting, [but also] stimulating and enriching visually, verbally, and with appropriate materials . . . and . . . as well, immediately and contingently responsive" (p. 47). The socially competent infant in turn, is ". . . the predictable, readable, responsive infant who has the potential of 'capturing' the initially unresponsive parent into cycles of effective interactions by generating parental feelings of efficacy," (Goldberg, 1977, p. 174).

Bromwich (1981) provides an excellent review of additional literature demonstrating the importance and mutuality of influence of a positive relationship between parent and child for all aspects of the child's development, including language. Bromwich sees interactions as a matter of "reciprocal reading and responding to each other's cues" which begins with bonding and attaching in the early months of life (p. 9). According to Bromwich, the normally developing infant's behaviors are seen as signals or cues by the parent who "reads" them and responds to them. The parent's behaviors eventually also become signals which the infant learns to read. It is through these early reciprocal transactions that the emotional ties or bonds are established which are crucial to the child's social-emotional, intellectual, and linguistic development. Bromwich says that the child is developing a rudimentary level of trust in the predictability of the human and physical environment, and in his ability to have some influence on it. The parent, in turn, is being "captured" by the infant as a storehouse of effective interactions is built up. For example, after the parent responds to the infant, he settles down, smiles, or babbles. These positive experiences can only serve to encourage both parent and infant to interact frequently, as both gain feelings of efficacy from it. As the infant develops socially and cognitively, the interactions become more complex. Eventually the child is motivated to use verbal language as a more effective means of dealing with the complexity and sophistication of the interactions.

Bromwich's intervention program for at-risk infants is based on this model of parent-infant interactions, and on the fact that the success of the process is entirely dependent upon the readability of each interactant's cues, as well as their sensitivity to each other's cues. When the cues of either are not easily read, or one seems to be unresponsive to the other, it may begin a downward spiral in the affective and interactive relationship between parent and infant. The parent becomes the focus of the intervention in this situation since it is the parent who has the potential of conscious control of his or her actions toward the infant. The intention is to help the parent perceive the infant's difficult-to-read cues and to modify parental responses in such a way that the infant's cues become more predictable, and the likelihood is increased that the infant will respond to the adult's behavior. Thus the downward spiral in the relationship would be reversed as the quality and mutuality of the interactions are enhanced—all of which favors optimal social-emotional, intellectual, and linguistic development of the infant.

The Child's Development of Interactional Abilities

Perhaps because widespread interest in children's development of language and communication abilities is a relatively recent phenomenon, there is at present a tangled confusion in terminology. One source of confusion is that the behaviors of very young infants have been described in terms formerly reserved only for linguistic behaviors (Bates, 1976; Bates, Camaioni, and Volterra, 1975; Bateson, 1979; Freedle and Lewis, 1977; Jaffe, Stern, and Peery, 1973; Trevarthen, 1977). The multiple application of terms contributes to questions about whether or not there is a continuity between preverbal and verbal behaviors; whether or not preverbal behaviors are precursors, prerequisites, or simply antecedents for verbal behaviors; and once again, the degree of importance which should be attributed to biological development and caregiver/environmental influences. (See, for example, the book edited by R. Golinkoff, 1983.) Bloom (1983) says child behaviors occurring prior to the child's use of spoken language share some features with spoken language behaviors. For example, the shared affective environment and timing of the "dance" of interactive behaviors in the very early months has features in common with the notion of reciprocal synchronization which occurs in verbal conversations. And the child's first words tend to be words about characteristics, movement, and locations of objects—the very concepts about which the prelinguistic child gradually acquires knowledge. But this relatedness or similarity should not be construed as implying that the linguistic behaviors necessarily develop out of the prelinguistic behaviors. For example, the child does not use speech *because* he has learned to babble; he does not talk about objects and their relationships *because* he has developed knowledge of them; and he does not communicate verbally *because* he can communicate nonverbally. On the other hand, as Sugarman (1983) says:

> Some preverbal experiences and acquisitions may nonetheless be critical to some aspects of language development. For example, it may be that unless children have learned something about communication prior to speaking they would have little motivation to look for a language to learn. . . . (p. 136)

To the careful observer, early infant behavior and learning (birth to twelve months) seem to be "all of a piece." Attempts to describe it impose artificial structure, uniformity, and order on what is actually a very complex, dynamic, and interwoven phenomenon. Added to that are the possibly erroneous inferences resulting from the widespread application of linguistic terminology to preverbal behaviors. The reader should be aware that, lacking a better way, the following discussion is guilty on both counts: it divides infant communication-learning into three (untidy) areas for consideration, and it uses the same widely accepted terminology.

It appears that the preverbal learning having the clearest relationship to later verbal learning has to do primarily with the establishment of the social structure and communicative groundwork, rather than with the semantic/syntactic groundwork (Kaye and Charney, 1980). Three features of discourse structure which are learned preverbally include joint reference to objects and events, turn-taking conventions, and the signalling of intention.

Joint Reference

One of the fundamental rules of fluent communication requires that the interactants share a focus or topic about which the message(s) is/are sent and received. For very young children, gaze and gesture are two of the means through which mutual attention is established and regulated (Bates et al., 1975; Collis and Schaffer, 1975; Stern 1974). It is generally believed that it is through gaze and gesture that the child eventually acquires an understanding that part of communicating involves the establishment of topics, and the means by which to establish them. Initially, the "jointly referenced focus" may be a "me-and-you" affiliative event as the mother and newborn engage in the patterns of mutual gazing and mother vocalizing/verbalizing described by Bateson (1979). Then, as the child begins to notice objects, colors, and movement, the mother frequently follows the child's direction of regard and comments on what the child is presumably observing (Bruner, 1975; Collis and Schaffer, 1975). By about four to six months of age (Scaife and Bruner, 1975), the child can follow the mother's gaze and will do so even more readily if the mother has just said something such as "Oh, look!" Over time, as the child begins to understand more and more spoken language (albeit initially within much-practiced routines), the mother can increasingly establish topics using verbal means alone.

The "gesture complex" is described by Bates, Benigni, Bretherton, Camaioni, and Volterra (1979) as follows. At about nine months of age, the child sometimes points at objects in the process of inspecting or examining them. This is not considered to be communicative. However, the child also now exhibits a "showing" gesture, whereby the child holds out an object for someone else to look at. This is considered to be communicative in that another person's involvement is essential, which is often signified by the child's looking toward the adult's face. This "showing" may or may not be accompanied by vocalizing. Soon after, the child not only shows the object to others, but actually allows the other to take it (i.e. the "giving" gesture). By about eleven months, the child points to objects in communicative fashion—not necessarily to obtain them, but just to point them out. Similar to the previous gestures, the child's pointing is most likely to be effective in obtaining and maintaining the other person's attention if it is accompanied by vocalizing. Interestingly, Carpenter, Mastergeorge, and Coggins (1983), observed that gestures were more and more frequently accompanied by vocal behaviors from about ten months of age. However, they note that at fifteen months, most communications still included gestures. Lasky and Klopp (1982) extended this observation to include the time from one to three years of age. This area is one which needs further research, but present evidence suggests that gestures are very important in the communicative behaviors of normally developing children throughout the birth- to three-year-old age range under consideration.

Turn-Taking Conventions

Sacks, Schegloff and Jefferson (1974) express the notion that the primary unit of conversation is turn-taking. This view certainly has face validity in that the "back-and-forthness" of fluent verbal communication between adults is clearly manifest. Fluent communicators know their culture's conventions regarding aspects of turn-taking such as: When in the flow of the other person's talk that it is permissable and/or expected that one should take a turn. They also know how to signal that they are finished, and that it is the other person's turn to talk. This is acquired knowledge, presumably learned in the course of the multitudinous interactive exchanges that the infant begins experiencing at birth. Kaye and Wells (1980), for example, have hypothesized that even the "jiggle-suck" sequence as the infant is nursed may be an initial kind of turn-taking prototype. Snow (1977) has observed that, in conversations with a young child, the adult's primary purpose seems to be to try to get the child to take a turn.

There are a number of characteristics in adult interactions with young children that could be interpreted as part of an effort to get the child to take a turn. For example, adults respond to the child with great consistency [see Chapter 3, p. 33, "Responsiveness"]. This could be seen as simple reinforcement of the child's behavior in the hope that the adult response will cause the child's behavior to be repeated, or even as a kind of modelling of responsive behavior in the hope that it eventually will be emulated by the child. In relation to adult-child vocalizing, Bates, O'Connell, and Shore (1987) note that an infant can return a "vocal volley" by about two months of age, and can initiate vocally by three to four months of age. They consider that true vocal imitation begins at about five months, but is not frequent or systematic until about ten months of age. During all of this time, the adult consistently initiates and responds to the child's behaviors (including a number of nonvocal behaviors), and thus frames the exchanges so that they seem to be conversational. Adults also make frequent attempts to engage the child in conversation, and adult speech to young children includes a large proportion of speech acts (e.g. expansions, questions, and requests) that are intended to elicit responses from the child (Bloom, Rocissano, and Hood, 1976; Brinton and Fujiki, 1982; Kaye, 1982; Kaye and Charney, 1980; Scherer and Olswang, 1984). In fact, all of the "motherese" alterations adults make in speaking to young children can be viewed as at least partly related to the adult's efforts to keep the child involved in the turn-taking process, (See p. 31, "Participation-Elicitors").

It is probably through such repeated interactive experiences that the child gradually acquires a knowledge of when to take a turn, as well as how to signal that the other person can take a turn. Rutter and Durkin (1987) have noted mastery of "terminal gaze" in children by twenty-four months of age. Terminal gaze is the common practice (in speakers in mainstream North American culture) of looking up at the listener at the end of a message to signal that the floor is about to be offered. When this practice has become part of the child's repertoire (apparently at twenty-four months of age), the turn-taking proceeds smoothly, with few interruptions of the other by either partner. However, the adult continues to take a leading (albeit gradually lessening) role in maintaining conversations with young children at least through three years of age, (Foster, 1985; Kaye, 1982; Kaye and Charney, 1980; Martlew, 1980; Rutter and Durkin, 1987; Wanska and Bedrosian, 1985.)

Signalling of Intention

The third preverbal development that seems critical to the acquisition of language is the intention to convey an idea or message to someone else. What follows is a description of hypothesized major milestones in the child's development of intentionality. The sequence is based on a proposal in Harding (1983), with additions from others (Bates et al., 1987; Sugarman, 1984). This way of viewing the developmental process for communicative intentionality has particular intuitive appeal, in that it requires the involvement of both partners for its definition and its acquisition.

In the first few months of life, the child's actions are oriented in simple unitary fashion toward either a person or an object. What the child does is grasp, drop, mouth, manipulate, or look at *either* a person or an object. It is widely agreed that these very early infant behaviors are not intentionally communicative. But, in that they quite consistently elicit reactions from the parent, they are viewed as having communicative effect. Soon, by about four months of age, some infant behaviors occur repetitiously or with persistence and the parent begins to infer that the behaviors are communicative. The simple unitary actions become more complex as they are used in tandem with one another to achieve a goal (e.g. child looks at toy, reaches for it, grasps it, and finally pulls it to his mouth). Adult interpretation of this goal-directed behavior as communicative is increasingly frequent between four and eight months of age. During this time, also, the parent consistently responds to the child's vocalizations as if they were meaningful conversation. Gradually, the child begins to expect certain behaviors of the adult to follow particular behaviors of his. He might be viewed as beginning to make inferences of his own about which of his behaviors cause particular adult behaviors to follow. Eventually, by about eight to ten months, the child combines an action toward an object with an action toward a person, such as looking at the mother while reaching for a toy. The child is now using people to get objects, as well as using objects to get attention from people, rather than acting on either objects or people separately. That is, rather than simply persisting in reaching toward a hard-to-attain toy, the child now reaches **as well as** looks at the mother; or looks back and forth between the two. This is considered to be a major milestone in the child's communicative development: the beginning of the child's encoding of intent for someone else; the first visible demonstration of the child purposefully conveying a message to another. The reaching and looking is soon combined with simultaneous vocalizing and more conventionalized gesturing such as pointing. In her research, Sugarman (1984) has observed that spontaneous use of words began just after coor-

dinated object and person behaviors were being used with some frequency. From then on, to oversimplify, the developmental process
basically consists of an increasing proportion of verbal [rather than
nonverbal] communications, and increasing length and complexity of
communicative episodes.

This description of the development of the discourse structures of
joint reference, turn-taking, and communicative intentionality provides a complementary framework for Bloom's notion regarding separately developing threads of abilities which converge at transition
points. Add to this the warm, responsive, nurturant affective environment, and the language-learning scene is nearly complete. The
missing piece is a description of the nature of parent talk in responding to the child, and/or in initiating interaction with him or her. Since
caregiver interactive behaviors may be one of the most important
elements of the child's language-learning environment (as well as one
of the most eligible for modification), they will be described in some
detail.

Characteristics of Caregiver Talk

Mothers (and others) have a special manner or register that they use
when talking to infants and young children at least from birth to age
three (Bellinger, 1980; Broen, 1972; Brown, 1973; Cross, 1977, 1978;
DePaulo and Bonvillian, 1978; Newport et al., 1977; Phillips, 1973;
Snow, 1972, 1977; Snow and Ferguson, 1977). Features of this "Baby
Talk" or "motherese" register are described below, as they appear in
the talk of mainstream North American mothers to their children.
Not surprisingly, the degree of the mother's incorporation of the
various features in her talk changes as the child moves from birth to
three years of age. Specific mention of changes is made within the
discussion of particular features.

1. Content: What Gets Talked About?

The vast majority of topics in the mother's talk from birth to three
months tend to be about the child's feelings and experiences (e.g. the
infant's feeling happy, sad, sleepy, hungry, getting fed, getting dia-
pered, getting picked up) (Snow, 1977). Many of these utterances are
in the form of single word "greetings" such as **Hi, OK, Yes, Oh, Aw,
Sure, What, Well, Hm** (Kaye, 1980). The topics in the mother's talk

begin to shift after about three months of age, so that by seven months of age, topics tend to be more evenly divided between the child's internal experiences and objects/events in the immediately surrounding environment. After seven months, there is a steady increase in the proportion of the mother's utterances about immediately present objects and people, actions presently occurring or actions just recently completed (Newport et al., 1977; Snow, 1977). With infants between eleven months and twenty-four months, Collis (1977) and Collis and Schaffer (1975) found 73 percent to 96 percent of the references to be about toys and objects which were actually being manipulated by either mother or child. This means, for example, that when the child is about one year of age, measures of motherese lexicon tend to yield sets of words reflecting the one-year-old's world. This is likely to include names of family members, and pets, terms of endearment, words for body parts and functions, words for basic qualities and conditions (e.g. pretty, dirty, good), names of toys and games (Ferguson, 1964).

The contingency between the topics in the mother's talk and the child's likely interests decreases sharply when the child begins using multiple word utterances (Bellinger, 1980; Cross, 1977; Cross, Johnson-Morris, and Nienhuys, 1980; Lasky and Klopp, 1982; Newport et al., 1977). It has been hypothesized that at that time, the adult senses that the child's cognitive and linguistic abilities are capable of supporting discussion of less immediate topics and events in the past and future.

The above discussion has been devoted to referential redundancy, or the parallel between the mother's verbal utterance and the child's interests in a particular context (sometimes also referred to as verbal-contextual redundancy). A related but somewhat different notion is that of the caregiver's semantic contingency. This refers to the tendency for the mother's utterances to be based on what the child is talking about. Research on parental semantic contingency shows that it correlates positively with children's progress in acquiring a number of language features. In fact, this is one of the most consistent and robust findings regarding motherese and its effects (Barnes, Gutfreund, Satterly, and Wells, 1983; Cross, 1978; Ellis and Wells, 1980; Nelson, 1973, 1981; Nelson, Carskaddon, and Bonvillian, 1973; Newport et al., 1977; Rocissano and Yatchmink, 1983). MacNamara (1972) has theorized that the key to a child's very early language acquisition (nonverbal or verbal) lies in the many situations where the immediately present focus of attention is encoded linguistically in the adult's utterance. The adult utterance thus provides "a great deal of syntactic and semantic information within a narrowly focused conversational frame" of the child's choosing (Lieven, 1984). This concept is closely related to Vygotsky's (1978) notion that higher mental functions, presumably including language, emerge in the child as a result of social mediation.

2. Phonology: What Does It Sound Like?

Relative to Adult-Adult speech, characteristic delivery in motherese tends to have higher overall pitch, more varied intonational contours, a slower pace, more rhythmic phrasing (it has been described as "sing-songy"), longer pauses between utterances, and clearer enunciation. Typical motherese also includes phonological simplification processes such as reduplication (e.g. the mother referring to the child's father as "Dada" in speaking to the child); and lengthened vowels (e.g. a prolonged "Hiiiiii!" or "You want some moooooooore?" (Broen, 1972; Newport, 1977; Phillips, 1973; Snow, 1972, 1977). Kaye (1980) found these phonological changes to be absent in mother's speech to infants at six and thirteen weeks of age. Another study, by Stern, Spieker, Barnett, and MacKain (1983), examined changes in maternal prosodic features at spaced intervals from the time the child was a newborn through two years of age. In contrast to Kaye (1980), at the four-month-old testing time, all of the measures of pitch and sound repetition showed more extensive or exaggerated use relative to the measures taken either before or after four months of age. Stern et al. suggest that this period of particularly exaggerated use may actually extend across the range from two to six months of age, and may be characteristic of this period of intense face-to-face play interaction. In this situation, the mother perceives her role as one of keeping the infant alert, interested, and happy. To carry out this role, she uses speech features that are most likely to get and hold attention such as a greater range of intonational contours, higher overall pitch, greater terminal and transitional pitch contrasts. The mother herself is often the focus of attention. As there are increases in the child's interest and ability to explore objects and to communicate about them, the mother's role shifts to facilitating those interests and abilities. For this new task, the pitch variation and sound repetition no longer need to be quite so exaggerated as they were when the mother was trying to get and keep the child's attention for face-to-face interactions. However they are still (even at two years) significantly different from Adult-Adult speech. This may be related to a continuing fairly frequent need to catch the child's attention, and/or to "cue" the child that he is being addressed, as suggested by Sachs (1979). It may also be part of an attempt to cue the child to take a turn, similar to pausing, as discussed in the next paragraph.

Maternal pausing between sequential utterances is greatest at birth and declines somewhat by two years of age. Arco and McCluskey (1981) and Stern et al. (1983) hypothesize that the elongated pauses are there to provide for the infant's slower processing time, as well as to arouse the infant, heighten affect, and to cue the child to take a turn. The need for long "invitational" pauses decreases somewhat after the basic turn-taking rules have been established, but the post-maternal-utterance pauses at two years of age are still approximately twice as long as they are in Adult-Adult conversation.

In contrast to that, however, most maternal responses to infants occur with a one-second interval (Beebe, Jaffe, Feldstein, Mays, and Alson, 1985; Schaffer, Collis, and Parsons, 1977; Stella-Prorok, 1983). And infants have also been found to respond to their mothers' utterances within a one-second interval (Beebe and Stern, 1977). It may be that, when the interaction is flowing smoothly, the turns are occurring regularly within a one-second interval of each other (Roth, 1987). But when the child is not responding for some reason, the mother simply increases the pause time before producing another utterance herself.

3. Semantics and Syntax: What About Complexity?

Compared with Adult-Adult talk, motherese to birth- to three-year-old North American children is generally shorter in length. Stern et al. (1983) found the mean length of the mother's utterances to infants between two days and two years of age to range from 3.12 to 4.58 morphemes. This was in contrast to a mean length of utterance to adults of 8.16. Phillips (1973) found a similar contrast of utterance length to infants and to adults (3.5 vs. 8.5 morphemes). In addition, motherese exhibits a restricted number of sentence types, as well as simplifications in both semantics (fewer semantic relations expressed in each utterance), and in syntax (fewer subordinate and coordinate clauses; fewer transformations, embeddings, conjoinings, function words).

Changes do occur in the complexity of the mother's semantics and syntax throughout the birth- to three-year-old period. However, there is marked disagreement among researchers concerning exactly which aspects change, when, in response to what, and in what manner. Snow, Perlman, and Nathan (1987) provide an excellent review of the confusion surrounding this issue. They provide a number of possible explanations for the conflict in research results. Some of the conflict may be related to the manner in which individual mothers adjust the complexity of their talk. For example, some mothers seem to match the child's mean length of utterance, and some stay four or five morphemes in advance of the child. This individual variation may or may not be taken into account in particular studies (Nelson, Bonvillian, Denninger, Kaplan, and Baker, 1984). Other possible sources of the conflict in research findings may be related to the types of situational contexts which were observed in the various experiments, as well as the need for longitudinal studies in order to explore the possibility that semantic/syntactic adjustments are made at one or more stages in the child's development, and not at others. Keeping in mind that this topic continues to need clarification, there does seem to be some consistency in two findings. The first is that the mother's syntax demonstrates the most change (increasing mean length of utterance) when the child is moving from eighteen to twenty-four months of age (Bellinger, 1979, 1980; Phillips, 1973). In contrast to that, the mother's use of semantic relations does not change at all during this period (Kaye, 1980; Retherford, Schwartz, and Chapman, 1981; and Snow, 1977).

4. Repetition: Say It or Play It Again

Two types of repetitions have been observed in mother's talk to infants. First, mothers immediately repeat their own utterances (in full) much more frequently in motherese than they do in talk to other adults (Broen, 1972; Kaye, 1980; Snow, 1972; Stern et al., 1983). This is especially true in the first months of life with an apparent peak in repetition at about four months of age where studies report 16 percent to 43 percent utterance repetition rates (Kaye, 1980; Stern et al., 1983; respectively). [See concurrent content and phonologic descriptions on pp. 24 and 26 above.] This repetitiveness gradually declines over the next two years to become more and more like that found in Adult-Adult conversation.

The other type of repetition has to do with the repeated occurrence of well-practiced sequences of exchanges or routines in interactions between mothers and young children. Research supports the importance of everyday routines and events as the context within which children learn socio-cultural values regarding appropriate modes of speaking and communicative conventions, as well as some specific lexical items and semantic/syntactic constructions. Much of this work is based on that of Bruner and his colleagues between 1975 and 1980. Bruner (1983) writes of mutual action formats or joint activities which are essential in order for the child to experience appropriate input in appropriate contexts. In essence, these are ordinary interactions where the adult and child do things with each other with a great deal of regularity. The responses of each are contingent upon the other's behaviors. In the North American context, these routines can be nursery rhymes, songs, tickling games, Peek-a-Boo games, book-reading, puzzle play, eating, bath, bedtime. The same (or nearly the same) words and phrases are used each time, which makes it easy for the child to predict the next move or utterance in the sequence. After several repetitions, the adult begins to expect child participation at appropriate moments. Less structured routines occur around a wide variety of daily events, where there can be subroutines embedded in longer-term routines. Here also, the patterned nature of the event helps the child discover how language is used (Conti-Ramsden and Friel-Patti, 1987; Lieven, 1984; Peters and Boggs, 1986; Snow, deBlauw and van Roosmalen, 1979; Snow and Goldfield, 1983; Snow et al., 1987).

5. Negotiation of Meaning: Huh?

Much of adult talk with young children can be described under the rubric of "attempts to negotiate meaning." In these instances, the adult is most often attempting to resolve the child's unclear, imprecise, incorrect, or incomplete utterance(s). At the same time, it is often the case that the adult's attempt to understand maintains the child's participation in the conversation (Snow, 1984a). Specific strategies which have been investigated can be classified as either clarification questions or as expansions (the latter are discussed on pp. 32–33).

Clarification questions or requests (or contingent queries) have been the focus of fairly extensive research interest. When the adult does not understand, he or she can attempt to resolve the child's meaning in one or more of the following ways:

a. Indicating lack of understanding through a puzzled facial expression and/or through gestures(s) such as lifting the arms and hands in a questioning manner. This can be done by itself, or in combination with any of the other clarification questions. (Peterson, Donner, and Flavell, 1972.)

b. Using a neutral request for repetition such as "What?," "Pardon?," "Huh?," "What did you say?," or "I didn't understand you." (Brinton and Fujiki, 1982; Gallagher, 1977, 1981; Gallagher and Darnton, 1978; Garvey, 1977.)

c. Using a yes/no (or "choice") question to solicit confirmation that the adult's interpretation is correct. Several varieties of these requests for confirmation occur:

(1) Adult simply repeats child's utterance with rising intonation.

Example

Context:	A toy teapot falls off the stove and turns upside down.
Child says:	"Look! Teapot turn up!" [articulation unclear]
Adult says:	[guessing] "Teapot turn up?"

(2) Adult repeats the child's utterance with rising intonation, as above, but also with semantic and/or syntactic elaboration.

Example

[Same context]

Child says:	"Look! Teapot turn up!"
Adult says:	"The teapot turned upside down?"

(3) Adult repeats part of the child's utterance with rising intonation.

Example

[Same context]

Child says:	"Look! Teapot turn up!"
Adult says:	"Up?"

(Gallagher, 1981; Garvey, 1977; also similar to "verbal reflectives" in McDonald and Pien, 1982; Olsen-Fulero, 1982; Olsen-Fulero and Conforti, 1983.)

d. Requesting repetition of a specific constituent in the child's utterance, using a "wh-" question or "wh-" word to replace the constituent.

Example

[Same context]

Child says: "Look! Teapot turn up!"

Adult says: "*What* turned up?" (Note syntactic elaboration which is likely to occur here.)

  or: "The teapot *what?*"

(Brinton and Fujiki, 1982; Gallagher, 1981; Garvey, 1977.)

e. Requesting more information in a general way by saying something like "Tell me more about that," or "What else can you remember about that?"

(Garvey, 1977; Peterson et al., 1972.)

6. Participation-Elicitors: Let's (Keep) Talk(ing).

Snow (1977) has said that one of the primary goals in Adult-Child conversation seems to be to get the child to take a turn. Clearly, the effect of the requests for clarification (described above) is to do just that. But, in fact, any questioning could be expected to include that same participation-eliciting intent (McDonald and Pien, 1982). Naturally, other intents are also likely to be there, such as truly soliciting information. However, any adult utterance that is followed by certain nonverbal cues such as an expectant pause and/or adult facial expression and/or slight lean toward the child could be viewed as participation-eliciting in intention. This may, in fact, describe nearly all of the prosodically highly marked adult utterances in face-to-face interaction with infants during at least the first six months of life. Two types of adult utterances to children after they begin talking bear particular mention in this regard, since they have received much research and intervention attention. These are "acknowledgements" and "expansions."

Acknowledgements are utterances that acknowledge and/or accept the child's previous utterance without adding anything to it. This may take the form of simple confirmatory repetition of the child's utterance or it may be short phrases such as "Right," "Oh," "Um-hmm."

In certain instances, the effect of an acknowledgement may be to give the speaker (child) positive feedback regarding the utterance's truth value or clarity, and/or the child's success in communicating his idea. In any case, acknowledgements tend to serve as an encouragement to the child's continued participation in the conversation (Cross, 1984; Ellis and Wells, 1980; Furrow, Nelson, and Benedict, 1979; Newport, 1977; Snow, Midkiff-Borunda, Small, and Proctor, 1984).

Expansions are adult utterances that incorporate part or all of the child's previous utterance in a syntactically and/or semantically better-formed sentence. Howe (1981) has made an important distinction between expansions which are either "minimal" or "extended." Minimal expansions fulfill the conversational requirement of replying to the speaker, and no more. They provide an improved or corrected alternative way of saying whatever the child said. Extended expansions likewise provide the improved or corrected alternative, but in addition, amplify the topic in some way. Extended expansions can request or provide new information about the same topic, or can apply the same information to a new topic.

Examples

Child says: "Zak." [as child taps dog's bowl with his foot].

   Minimal expansion: "Yes, it's Zak's."

   [N.B. Minimal expansions tend to be primarily syntactic.]

   Extended expansion: "Yes, it's Zak's bowl, and
                              it's empty."

                       or

                       "Yes, it's Zak's bowl, and
                        this is Zak's toy.'

   [N.B. Extended expansions provide both syntactic and semantic additions.]

Howe's research results are inconclusive concerning the possible advantages of one type of expansion over the other, and the intention of her research was not to provide practical suggestions. However, the differential effects of minimal versus extended expansions bear further investigation (particularly longitudinally) since the intuitive implications seem obvious. That is, it might be expected that the extended expansions could, at least at some stages in the child's development, be useful as a language-promoting strategy. Furthermore, research which examined the effects differentially might shed light on the unreconciled conflict between Cazden's results (reported in Brown, Cazden, and Bellugi-Klima, 1969) that expansions were not helpful, and the findings of Nelson et al. (1973) that they were.

In any case, (generic) expansions of child utterances may be one of the most frequently suggested and employed strategies in language intervention settings. Their use is based on observations that expansions occur frequently in normal caregiver talk (Barnes et al., 1983; Cross, 1977; Ellis and Wells, 1980; Furrow et al., 1979; Nelson, 1973; Nelson et al., 1976; Newport et al., 1977). Research has also shown that children are most likely to imitate expansions over any other type of adult utterance (Folger and Chapman, 1978; Scherer and Olswang, 1984; Seitz and Stewart, 1975). It may be that an expansion has particular salience (i.e. it stands out clearly) and motivating value for a child since it is based directly on the child's utterance, and simply introduces an element of relevant, moderate novelty to it. These two aspects of expansions (that they are motivating, and that they provide information about alternative ways of expressing things) may explain the strong positive correlations found by some researchers (cited above) between expansions and measures of language gain. (Note that this explanation may also be applicable to several of the clarification request categories.)

7. Responsiveness

In face-to-face interactive play, mothers tend to be very consistently responsive to their children's behaviors (Brazelton, Koslowski, and Main, 1974; Newson, 1977; Snow, 1977; Stern, 1974; Trevarthen, 1977). As Kaye and Charney (1980) describe the situation in the very early months, ". . . the rule seems to be that if an infant gives his mother any behavior which can be interpreted as if he has taken a turn in a conversation, it will be; if he does not, she will pretend he has" (p. 227). This fits well with Harding's conception of the development of intentionality in the infant. As the infant's cognitive, communicative, and sensori-motor abilities increase, the mother becomes more selective about what she will accept as a communicative behavior or conversational turn from the child (Newson, 1977, Snow, 1977; Snow et al., 1979). That is, when the child is between birth and three months of age, the mother will respond to his every burp, sneeze, yawn, cough, cry, smile, gaze, and minimal vocalization (coos and goos) as if they were actual conversational contributions.

Example

Context:	Mother holding two-month-old baby on shoulder after child has nursed; mother is patting baby on back gently.
Mother:	"Ok . . . . Time for burpies. Ok now . . . . Yeah! Soooo full . . .. Yes, you are. Yeah . . . . What a baby! Um-hmmmm. . . ."
Baby:	[burps]
Mother:	"Oooh! Wow! What a big burp! Good job! Yes. . . . Now you feel better."

The parent incorporates the child's behaviors in such a way that a semblance of dialogue is created even in these very early encounters.

Starting when the child is about seven months of age, the mother begins to require a bit more from the child in terms of vocalizations and motoric behaviors before she will accept them as conversational turns. She will still often respond to smiles, laughs, burps, and crying as if they were turns, but the vocalizations now tend to be ignored unless they include some consonantal or vocalic babble. The mother is also now more likely to ignore simple kicking or arm flailing. She will respond more selectively to more advanced motoric behaviors such as taking a bite of food, looking toward an object after it has moved or been talked about, or reaching for an object. These requirements for more sophisticated behaviors clearly reflect the mother's recognition of the child's increasing abilities. Through the seven-month to thirty-six-month period, the mother continues to "up the ante" in terms of requiring communicative behaviors from the child. The child's developing abilities and the maternal requirements run parallel to each other, so that the mother continues to be quite consistently responsive to a large proportion of the child's behaviors throughout the birth- to three-year-old age range. And, in fact, research has shown that the frequency of parental acceptance of utterances (in the form of acknowledgements and interjections) is positively associated with children's language acquisition (Ellis and Wells, 1980; Furrow et al., 1979; Newport, 1977).

The work of Kaye and Charney (1980, 1981) extends this discussion of responsiveness one step further. Their study of early mother-infant discourse is based on the Fillmore analogy (1973, cited in Kaye and Charney, 1981) that the back-and-forth cycles in conversation are similar to a game of catch. A competent participant in either event both catches and throws with ease. The type of interactional turn (verbal and/or nonverbal) which both: (a) responds to the previous turn by the partner, and (b) attempts to elicit a response from the partner has been called a "turnabout" by Kaye and Charney. Turnabouts seem to be more frequent in adult talk to children than to other adults, and the mothers in Kaye and Charney's studies did turnabouts two to three times more frequently than the children. Turnabouts are considered to be very powerful language-learning devices, since a turnabout by the mother has the properties of relating directly to the child's previous topic, of being responsive to it, and also of positing an expectation of further response from the child. It should be noted that turnabouts may take the form of any of the utterance types described above as being used for negotiation of meaning and/or for eliciting the child's participation. Mothers respond initially to very minimal child behaviors as if they were conversationally meaningful. In catching such minimal behaviors *and* tossing the conversational ball back, the mother is creating a situation where the child appears to be much more of an active participant than he may actually be. Interestingly, of course, the child eventually *does* become an active participant. This process certainly has all the markings of a self-fulfilling prophecy!

Motherese: Why?

The period from birth to three years of age is marked by consistent maternal responsiveness and the framing of interactive events toward the appearance of more and more sophisticated conversations. This creates a situation of some contrast between Adult-Adult and Adult-Child conversation. This seems to fit with Snow's (1977) contention that the purpose of Adult-Adult conversation appears to be to get to take a turn; in Adult-Child conversation, the purpose is to get the child to take a turn. There is a special significance to this differentiation as it has become one of the primary explanations for why adults "do" motherese. The adult's accepting minimally meaningful behaviors from the child as communicative, is seen as part of an effort to provide a conversational frame to the encounter, and facilitate the child's participation in the "dialogue" (Barnes et al., 1983; Bruner, 1977; Martlew, 1980; Newport et al., 1977; Snow, 1977; Wanska and Bedrosian, 1985). The adult's frequent use of imitations of the child's productions, continuates, invitations to vocalize, and "turnabouts" (Kaye and Charney, 1980, 1981) all provide additional supportive evidence of this adult effort toward guaranteeing conversational flow.

Another widely held view of the reason why adults use the motherese register is the "feedback" or "fine-tuning" explanation. The notion is that the modifications are tailored to meet the child's developing linguistic and attention levels (Bellinger, 1979, 1980; Cross, 1977; Cross and Johnson-Morris, 1980; Cross, Johnson-Morris, and Nienhuys, 1980; Phillips, 1973; Snow, 1972). Support for this explanation arises from two factors: (1) the increasingly stringent maternal expectations for quality, conventionality, and complexity in the child's communicative behaviors, and (2) the increasing complexity occurring in the nature of the topics, vocabulary, semantics, and syntax in the mother's language. The changes observed in the mother's talk are seen as motivated by her sensitivity to what the child can or cannot comprehend. Her talk is continually adjusted in order to maintain an optimal fit between what the child deals with linguistically and that to which the mother exposes him. The mother thus uses motherese primarily to ensure the effectiveness of her message-sending in terms of the child's understanding and learning. Naturally, this would also enhance the chances of the child's participating in the conversation which suggests that the feedback and conversation-promoting motivations for motherese are ultimately not so dissimilar.

Other explanations for the motherese register are that it is used to convey a warm, loving, nurturing affect (Sherrer, 1974); to make oneself and one's talk interesting to the child in order to attract and maintain the child's attention (Kaye, 1980; Sachs, 1977; Snow, 1972); to help the child learn specific linguistic items and vocabulary (DePaulo and Bonvillian, 1978; Furrow et al., 1979; Gleitman, Newport, and Gleitman, 1984). Kaye (1980) has also suggested another explanation for the nature of the mother's talk to infants. In examining the substance of the mother's talk as she shapes the interaction to look like a dialogue, it appears as if the mother is trying construct a theory about who the baby is: the baby's intentions, motives, sentiments, perceptions, beliefs. (See Kaye [1980, p. 503] for an excellent example.) These efforts on the mother's part are seen as governed by her expectations of the baby as a person, and by her beliefs about how one is supposed to interact with a baby.

All of these explanations have theoretical explanatory merit for at least some features of motherese at some steps in the developmental process: the explanations are complementary, rather than in conflict.

Motherese: Immaterial or Facilitative?

While no one disputes the fact that absent or greatly impoverished adult input has a devastating effect on language-learning, there is much disagreement about the nature of the adult input that is necessary and/or facilitative of language development in normally developing children. Researchers have not been especially successful at establishing robust relationships between particular semantic, syntactic, or pragmatic features of motherese and subsequent language growth for normal language learners. (See reviews in Hoff-Ginsberg and Shatz [1982] and Snow et al. [1987].) As Snow et al. (1987) say, "Almost any conclusion could be justified by referring to one or more . . . studies. . . ." (p. 72).

One of the sources of confusion is the well-documented individual variability in maternal interactional styles (Kaye, 1980; Kaye and Charney, 1980, 1981; Lieven, 1978a, 1984; McDonald and Pien, 1982; Olsen-Fulero, 1982; Snow, et al, 1987; Tiegerman and Siperstein, 1984). There is a continuum of maternal interactional styles often referred to in the literature which has a child-centered style at one extreme and an adult-centered style at the other. The child-centered style includes many of the features described above in their most supportive, responsive, and nurturing forms, and has been shown to be facilitative of language development (e.g. Cross, 1978; Furrow et al., 1979; Nelson, 1973; Newport et al., 1977). This is in contrast to the adult-centered style, which has much in common with characteristics of caregiver talk to children with language-learning problems (See Chapter 4), and which has been shown to inhibit language development (Clarke-Stewart, 1973; Cross, 1978; Nelson, 1973; Newport et al., 1977). The clarity of this dichotomized scheme has a certain simplistic appeal. However, in a closer examination of the data on caregiver styles by Olsen-Fulero (1982), a different categorization emerged, as did at least one additional factor to investigate. One major category, "mothers who are trying to influence the child," included the continuum of child-centered to adult-centered styles already described. The other major category was for "mothers who were trying to instruct the child." The new factor to consider was a measure of informality and warmth which seemed to discriminate further amongst the already identified categories. A different, but possibly related approach to this issue is provided by Howe's (1981) differentiation amongst recursive, excursive, and discursive styles. Clearly, individual variability in caregiver styles needs further research investigation. In the meantime, interventionists will need to temper their pronouncements with a healthy respect for the tentative scientific basis of it all.

Other sources of variability and confusion are related to the contexts being observed in studies of interacting (Conti-Ramsden and Friel-Patti, 1987; Snow et al., 1987) and to changes identified in characteristics of the mother's style at different developmental stages of the child (Bellinger, 1980). And this is not even touching on the nature of the influence on the mothers of differences in the *children's* cognitive, learning, and/or interactive style and temperaments (e.g. Bates et al., 1987; Cross, 1977, 1981; Cross and Johnson-Morris, 1980; Garnica, 1977; Nelson, 1973, 1981).

As if this were not enough confusion, cross-cultural studies (e.g. Crago, 1988; Ochs and Schieffelin, 1979; Schieffelin and Eisenberg, 1984) demonstrate that children can become competent language users without experiencing the same adult adjustments typical of middle-class motherese in English. However, it is difficult to entertain the notion that all of those well-documented motherese adjustments are irrelevant, at least for children learning language in middle-class English-speaking culture. It seems possible that the importance of motherese may be obscured by the application of traditional experimental methodologies and their underlying philosophical orientations to social interaction research in this culture (Sugarman, 1983; Van Kleek, 1985). That is, it seems possible that we are not asking the questions, and/or gathering and analyzing the data in ways which will allow the relevant information to emerge. Research studies need to account for the general variability of individual caregiver styles, for the variability related to the contexts and cultures observed and to developmental changes in the child, as well to differences in the child's cognitive, learning, and/or interactive style and temperament.

It also seems possible that the language-learning process for the normally developing child is well-cushioned by the child's intact "intake" and "output" systems, and perhaps by the strength of hypothesized drives toward being like his parents or toward communicating in the most efficacious manner possible. The normal child will probably develop language in the face of a number of adverse conditions. For the child with hearing impairment (similar to any child with language learning problems), however, the cushioning is not there. There seems to be more need for an optimal set of conditions in order for the child to reach his maximal level of achievement (Snow et al., 1984; Lieven, 1984; Rice, 1986). This, and its implications for intervention, will be further explored in Chapter 4.

This chapter's detailed discussion presents state-of-the-art information regarding the major elements involved in the normal language-learning scene between birth and three years of age. This has been provided in keeping with the perspective that, given an adequately stimulating auditory, communicative, and linguistic environment, nearly all hearing-impaired children can be expected to follow the normal sequence of spoken language development. As has always been the case, interventionists will need to exercise caution and common sense in the application to particular cases of our perpetually incomplete scientific knowledge.

3

Interactions Between Caregivers and Hearing-Impaired Children

God could not be everywhere, so [she] created [caregivers].
(Folk saying, mildly paraphrased)

Potential Effects of Hearing Loss on Interactions

Sometimes a child's hearing loss seems to have little or no effect on the interactive relationship with his or her parents. But the intactness of those interactions **can** be threatened in several ways. First of all, when a child has an undetected hearing loss, he is not receiving auditory-linguistic stimulation in the manner that his normally hearing peers are receiving it. And even after a sensori-neural loss is detected and appropriate hearing aids worn consistently, the input is reduced in quality and quantity. That is, the hearing aid is unlike corrective lenses for eyes: it does not make listening abilities normal, it simply makes the sounds louder. Speech still lacks the clarity and intensity of the speech received by a normally hearing infant. Further, the child with a severe-to-profound hearing loss cannot benefit from "over-

41

hearing" conversations directed toward others in his environment in a manner similar to his normal hearing peers (Ling, 1981). These are the physiologically based reasons that the process of learning spoken language can be so long and arduous for hearing-impaired children. These are also reasons that the child with a hearing loss may not respond in expected ways to parent messages or cues, and may not send out expected cues. This mismatch of expectations can disrupt interactional events from the very beginning. In addition, the caregiver's ability to interact "normally" may also be influenced by emotional turmoil which can surround the discovery, as well as the continuing presence, of the hearing loss. The vast majority of parents of children with newly detected hearing loss come to the event with healthy emotional/psychological histories. However, discovery of the loss can be an emotionally cataclysmic event. One normal response is to go through various stages of a kind of grieving process, while gradually learning to adjust and cope (Moses, 1979; Luterman, 1979, 1984, 1987; Shontz, 1965). In the course of this process, a number of powerful emotions are experienced by the parent that may interfere with the parent's normal ability to be sensitive to the child's communicative cues, to respond to them, and to send appropriate cues to the child.

In addition, there are frustrations and problems inherent to trying to understand and be understood by any young child who is only just beginning to learn that adult signals (e.g. words) have consistency and significance. If the child is the physical size of a two-and-a-half year old with normal cognitive abilities, but is understanding and producing language at a much younger age level, this does **not** reduce the frustrations and problems.

To summarize, the lack of expected audition-based responses from the child, the slowness of the process due to the reductions in quality and quality of the auditory-linguistic input, and the parent's emotional turmoil all may contribute toward limiting the child's access to precisely the kind of auditory, linguistic, and social interaction that he or she needs. Further, these factors may explain some of the research findings regarding caregiver talk to hearing-impaired children.

Research Findings

The predominant finding in studies of communication between caregivers and children with hearing impairment is that the mothers' speech to these children varies considerably from the norm. This finding supports the "feedback" explanation for motherese which says that the caregiver's talk is adjusted because of cues received from the child regarding levels of comprehension and attention. Some of the differences found in caregiver talk to hearing-impaired children include decreased amount of talk (Cross, 1977; Gregory, Mogford, and Bishop, 1979; Lieven, 1978a), more exact self-repetitions (Gregory et al., 1979; Wedell-Monnig and Westerman, 1977), fewer expansions (Cross, Nienhuys, and Morris, 1980; Nienhuys, Cross, and Horsborough, 1984); shorter Mean Length of Utterance (MLU) and simpler grammatical constructions (Cross, Johnson-Morris, and Nienhuys, 1980; Cross, Nienhuys, and Morris, 1980; Gregory et al., 1979; Matey and Kretschmer, 1985; Wedell-Monnig and Westerman, 1977).

Two exceptions to the studies yielding differences from the norm, are studies by Anderson (1979) and Blennerhasset (1984). Both found that, similar to the normal situation, caregivers frequently engaged in reciprocal turn-taking with their young hearing-impaired children. The interpretation is that the caregivers were viewing the hearing-impaired child as a conversational partner, and were attempting to structure the event into one of back-and-forth exchange.

These findings and explanations are not necessarily in conflict with each other. The adult speaking to a hearing-impaired child may very well intend to create a semblance of dialogue and of getting the child to take a turn in a communicative exchange—just as the adult would with a normally hearing child. But, the adult may also be simultaneously searching for cues regarding the child's understanding of what is being said. The adult may determine that the hearing-impaired child has not understood, and consequently may automatically shift into a form of motherese similar to what the adult might use with a younger normally hearing child. This is likely to include somewhat shorter sentences, more repetitions, and simpler grammatical constructions. The adult's talk would thus have been different to the hearing-impaired child versus his hearing same-age peer, but not unlike the motherese likely to appear with a younger, less linguistically sophisticated child with normal hearing. This seems to be the case in studies with hearing-impaired and language-impaired children who have been matched with control groups based on linguistic ability rather than on chronological age (Conti-Ramsden and Friel-Patti, 1983;

Cross, Nienhuys, and Kirkman, 1982; Lasky and Klopp, 1982; Nienhuys et al., 1984; Peterson and Sherrod, 1982).

In view of the observed difference in adult talk to hearing-impaired children, several other frequently observed research findings bear further consideration. One is that motherese to children with language-learning problems (including those related to hearing impairment) tends to include more frequent rejecting, critical, negative, inhibiting, or ignoring responses than motherese to normally developing children (Cross, 1984; Greenstein, Greenstein, McConville, and Stellini, 1975; Schlesinger and Meadow, 1972). It seems possible that these may occur because the child's utterances are less often understandable. Consequently, the parents have fewer **opportunities** to accept and be approving of them. There are times in the development of some "normal" children when the child's articulation ability lags behind his language ability, and he or she is likely to say things the mother cannot understand or guess correctly. It would be interesting to investigate the degree of negativity in motherese occurring in response to normally developing children specifically at a time period when their spoken language is lacking in intelligibility and predictability (e.g. twenty to thirty months). It may be that the negativity of mothers of hearing-impaired children appears to last longer or be more prevalent than that of normally developing children simply because the children's unintelligibility lasts longer.

Another related and frequently observed finding about motherese to children with language-learning problems is that it tends to include much more frequent direct imperatives than motherese to normally developing children (Bellinger, 1980; Brinich, 1980; Cross, 1978; Cross, Nienhuys, and Morris, 1980; Clarke-Stewart, 1973; Furrow et al., 1979; Gregory et al., 1979; Martin, 1981; Nienhuys et al., 1984; Nelson, 1973; Snow, 1977; Wedell-Monnig and Lumley, 1980; White and White, 1984; Wood, 1982). That is, the parents are frequently telling the children what to do and attempting to control their behavior. Not surprisingly, there is a concomitant finding that these parental directives frequently change the topic **away from** the child's focus of attention, activity or previous utterance (Cross, 1984; Rocissano and Yatchmink, 1983). Furthermore, most of these studies have also shown a negative relationship between frequency of adult imperatives and topic changes, and measures of the child's language development. However, the meaning of these results is uncertain since most of these studies were not longitudinal. They did not, for example, continuously cover the ages of ten months through three years. Consequently the possibility exists that there may be stages in normal development where the use of more frequent imperatives is entirely appropriate and useful. A number of studies already point in this direction (Barnes et al., 1983; Bellinger, 1980; Cross, 1977; Cross and Johnson-Morris, 1980; Cross, Nienhuys, and Morris, 1980; Ellis and Wells, 1980; Garnica, 1977; Nienhuys et al., 1984; White and White, 1984).

On the other hand, however "normal" negative parental responding and frequent imperatives may be, they merit particular concern in intervention with parents and their young hearing-impaired children. One reason is that both of these elements have been shown to be negatively correlated with measures of language acquisition, as cited above. The other reason to be concerned about these aspects is that their overall impact may be to create a parent-child environment which is primarily negative and directive in nature; hardly conducive to the child's growth in any area (Clarke-Stewart, 1973; Bromwich, 1981). If this is happening, it may be reflecting parental frustration and anger related to having a child with hearing impairment and language problems, and if so, those parental feelings need to be addressed as a separate part of the intervention. Clearly, the child with language-learning problems needs abundant positive reinforcement and praise for attempts to communicate, and also needs to experience a large measure of parental talk which is not simply ordering him about. **How much** of these elements is optimal will probably have to depend on an individual, context-based judgement.

Another of the research findings regarding motherese to children with language-learning problems may have a similar source; that is, may be internal to the parent. Several studies have shown that adult speech to children with language-learning problems is sometimes faster, less fluent, less intelligible, and less audible than speech to normally developing children (Cross, 1984; Schodorf, 1982). This may seem to be surprising in view of most adults' immediate adoption of slow and careful articulation in speaking to persons who seem to understand little. When the parent's speech is faster and less intelligible, it may be related to the fact that the parent has a long-term, on-going relationship with this particular child who understands little. The parent's fast-paced, quiet, and less carefully articulated speech may sound as if he or she is speaking to him or herself, which may very well be what the parent has begun to feel as if he or she is doing. That is, he or she may, based on repeated experience, have very little expectation that the child will understand no matter how carefully articulated the speech. If this is the case, parental feelings of hopelessness may need to be addressed as a separate part of the intervention. In any case, particularly with hearing-impaired children, it is vitally important that the speech addressed to the child be normally paced and audible, as well as clearly articulated.

One final research finding needs to be mentioned regarding motherese to children with language-learning problems. Snow et al. (1984) observed a high frequency of adult demands for imitation in situations where it was not necessarily communicatively useful for the children to imitate. This sounds likely to be related to a not-surprising desire on the part of the parent (or interventionist) to receive some indication that what has been said has been understood and/or learned by the child. And immediate imitation seems to provide that information, fallacious or not. Normally, a certain percentage of children do spontaneously imitate, apparently in order to keep a conversation going, to practice unfamiliar forms, and/or to learn new forms. But imitation is very selectively used by most children, and only for communicatively useful forms. In general, in ordinary conversations with children with or without language-learning problems, it would seem wise to respect these findings regarding individual variability and selectivity for imitation. However, there will undoubtedly be many times and occasions in intervention settings where expecting the child to imitate is the most efficacious way of checking on whether or not the child has, at least on some level, "processed" the message or input.

What All This Means

Clearly, the presence of a hearing loss in an infant can cause interactions between parent and child to be at risk for a number of reasons, and in a variety of ways. A less-than-optimal language-learning environment (e.g. haphazard caregiving, sporadic parental responsiveness) may not result in irreparable language problems for physiologically intact children (Snow et al., 1984), who seem to have reserves that buffer them against the potentially negative effects of such an environment. But a child with a sensory impairment such as severe-to-profound hearing loss could be viewed as having lost that buffering.

He may progress best with more frequent and direct access to social and verbal interactions, more consistent adult responsiveness, more repetition in varied ways, and more consciously planned input. As a consequence, it becomes imperative that the interventionist understand the features of optimal, growth-promoting interactions between parents and their young hearing-impaired children in order to foster them. The Checklist which follows is offered as an attempt to augment that understanding.[2]

Introduction to the Checklist

Purpose and Focus

This Checklist is intended to provide a framework from which to consider the appropriateness of the parent's role in communicative interactions with their young hearing-impaired child. This is done by identifying important features of normal, everyday caregiver-child interactions, and providing explanatory guidelines to use in understanding the feature's impact, as well as attempting to put them into practice.

The focus here is on the parent since it is the adult who has the ability to make conscious choices regarding his or her behavior with the infant. The expectation is that the interventionist will encourage the parent to choose behaviors which will enhance the quality and mutuality of the communicative interactions, and thus optimally support the child's potential for spoken language learning. The child's role is not the primary focus. However, in using the Checklist, the child's behaviors (both antecedent and subsequent to the adult's behaviors) need to be examined as they can shed light on the motivation for, as well as the effect of, the adult's behaviors.

Items on the Checklist are intended to outline the major components of optimal caregiver communication-promoting behaviors, with several additions specific to interacting with a hearing-impaired child. All of the items in Section I are related to being sensitive to the child in some way. This section is intended to highlight specific adult behaviors which can promote a positive affective environment. Section II of the

---

[2]The present form of the Checklist is a revised and elaborated version of Table 1 in Cole and St. Clair-Stokes (1984).

Checklist for Caregivers:
Communication-Promoting Behaviors

Name: _____

Completed by: _____

Date: _____

Rating scale for communication-promoting behaviors

Rarely observed   Often observed

1 ◄—— 2 —— 3 —— 4 —— 5 —— 6 —— ► 7

Behavior	Rating	Comments
I. Sensitivity to child		
1. Handles child in a positive manner.		
2. Paces play and talk in accordance with child's tempo.		
3. Follows child's interests much of the time.		
4. Provides appropriate stimulation, activities, and play for the child's age and stage.		
5. Encourages and facilitates child's play with objects and materials.		

II. Conversational behaviors

A. In responding to the child

6. Recognizes child's communicative attempts.

7. Responds to child's communicative attempts.

8. Responds with a response which includes a question or comment requiring a further response from the child.

9. Imitates child's productions.

10. Provides child with the words appropriate to what he/she apparently wants to express.

11. Expands child's productions semantically and/or grammatically.

B. In establishing shared attention

12. Attempts to engage child.

13. Talks about what child is experiencing, looking at, doing.

14. Uses voices (first) to attract child's attention to objects, events, self.

continued

Checklist for Caregivers:
Communication-Promoting Behaviors (*Continued*)

Behavior	Rating	Comments
15. Uses body movement, gestures, touch appropriately in attracting child's attention to objects, events, self.		
C. In general		
16. Uses phrases and sentences of appropriate length and complexity.		
17. Pauses expectantly after speaking to encourage child to respond.		
18. Speaks to child with appropriate rate, intensity, and pitch.		
19. Uses interesting, animated voice.		
20. Uses normal, unexaggerated mouth movements.		
21. Uses audition-maximizing techniques.		
22. Uses appropriate gesture.		

Checklist outlines the interactive mechanics of the situation: the "how" of establishing a shared focus, of responding, and of talking to the child. This section includes items from the language intervention literature which are believed to be facilitative of language development in children with language-learning problems. Further explanation of all components follows the Checklist.

How to Proceed

The Checklist is intended to be used in the study of videotaped samples of the parent and child interacting in a normal, everyday fashion. Videotaping is the method of choice for collecting the sample since it provides a retrievable record of both the auditory and visual components of the events. Since much early communicating occurs through nonvocal/nonauditory means such as changes in gaze direction, body orientation, and gesture, it is especially important to have the visual record available. Videotaping also allows for multiple reviewing of the interactional sample. This is necessary in order to account for social, physical, and linguistic dimensions of the context which contribute the interactants' co-construction of meaning in a given instance (Keller-Cohen, 1978; Mishler, 1979; Prutting, 1982).

The usefulness of the sample depends very heavily on the degree to which it is representative of normal interacting between this particular parent and child. Often the presence of the equipment and the observational aspects of the videotaping event itself mitigate against "naturalness." It is not unusual for the parent to feel a bit shy and embarrassed at the first taping session, or for either the parent or the child to "perform," sometimes unconsciously. Some of the following measures may be helpful in counteracting these possibilities and attempting to set everyone at ease so that the sample will be as representative as possible:

- Videotaping can take place in the child's home or in some other setting which is very familiar to the child.

- The interventionist can discuss the purpose and planned use of the tape with the caregiver. The purpose is to get a good sample of how the caregiver and child play and talk together, which will then be studied by both the interventionist and the parent to be certain that the interactions are as language- promoting as they can be. The caregiver's help can be enlisted in order to decide which toys or activities to have available for the taping (e.g. feeding or lunchtime; diaper-changing, bathing; playing in a swing; playing with play dough, tea set, dolls and clothes, building blocks, doctor kit, etc.).

- The interventionist can mention to the parent that he or she will be trying not to interact with either participant during the taping. The usefulness of the tape will be greatly compromised if much of the parent's talk is directed to the interventionist rather than to the child. It will also be compromised if the child is constantly looking off-camera at the interventionist, or walking over to him or her.

- The interventionist can set up the equipment, and then wait five or ten minutes before actually beginning the taping in order to let some of the novelty wear off. It will depend upon the particular child whether or not it is most useful to allow some (limited) exploration of the equipment, or simply not to allow the child to touch it.

- The videotaping should be at least ten or fifteen minutes in duration. Usually adults' camera consciousness abates after about five minutes; children often forget about the camera immediately if the activity holds enough interest for them. After that occurs, the sample of normal, natural, everyday interacting needs to be at least five to ten minutes in duration.

For each individual case, the interventionist will need to determine whether it is most useful to study and discuss the videotape with the parent immediately after making it, or to delay the mutual discussion until the interventionist has had a chance to study and analyze it independently. Numerical ratings can be applied to each item, or written comments made.

Procedures for using the Checklist as part of the intervention process are presented in Chapter 6.

Explanation for Items

I. Sensitivity to Child

Items in this section all require that the caregiver demonstrate a level of awareness of the child's way of being, and a desire to adjust to it in a supportive manner which promotes the child's social/emotional, cognitive, **and** linguistic development. The items can be grouped as follows.

Item #1: Affect

Handles child in positive manner. Research suggests that caregivers of children with language-learning problems tend to be critical, negative, and inhibiting as they interact with their children (Cross, 1984; Greenstein et al., 1975; Schlesinger and Meadow, 1972). If this is the case, it may be cause for serious concern since the parent-child affective relationship is considered to have fundamental importance for a child's language development, as well as for his or her social and cognitive development (Bromwich, 1981; Clarke-Stewart, 1973; Dore, 1986; Thoman, 1981). "Handling the child in a positive manner" could include behaviors such as caressing, hugging, smiling; and behaving in a warm, loving, accepting, and joyous fashion with the child. It could also include simply being near the child, watching him or her thoughtfully, and being openly available for interaction. The key question here is, "Does the parent behave in ways which tell the child that the parent loves him and enjoys being with him?"

Clearly, one person's making judgements about another's feelings for their child can be highly inappropriate and invasive—not to mention *wrong*! Chapter 6 suggests several possible ways to address this item with sensitivity and care. Sometimes, even if many other areas on the Checklist are problematic, this is one area that is not, and the importance of it can be emphasized by the interventionist. Sometimes it is a question of the caregiver not knowing how to behave in ways which send the warm, positive message they want to send. Sometimes the caregiver is unaware of the difference that this can make in the child's behavior. And sometimes the caregiver actually is feeling primarily frustrated, angry, or hopeless towards the child, rather than warm and loving. Obviously, this can be a temporary or long-term phenomenon. The interventionist must be aware of the limits of his or her expertise in addressing this particular area, and must know when to draw on the assistance of a social worker or clinical psychologist.

Items #2 and 3: Pacing and Focus

Paces play and talk in accordance with child's tempo; follows child's interests much of this time. These items relate to the caregiver's ability to read the child's cues regarding such dimensions as the amount of information and stimulation the child can absorb, and the rate at which he or she can do so; the kinds of things the child is interested in, and how he or she indicates that interest. Research suggests that caregivers of children with language-learning problems sometimes have difficulty getting a feel for their particular child's tempo (Cross, 1984; Schodorf, 1982). They also tend to bring up their own topics frequently, which are often attempts to control or inhibit the child's behavior, or to get him or her to imitate particular sounds or words (See citations in Chapter 2; also Cross, 1984; Rocissano and Yatch-mink, 1983). What needs to happen is for the caregiver to observe the child frequently and carefully, to follow his or her interests and tempo, and to fit in with both. With a young child, the cues may lie in such things as rate of body movement, orientation and/or tension of the body, facial expressions, gaze direction, gaze shifts, gestures, and vocalizations (Bateson, 1979; Bates et al., 1979; Carpenter et al., 1983; Lasky and Klopp, 1982; Scaife and Bruner, 1975).

The interventionist and the caregiver may find it useful to study the videotapes of the child interacting to determine what the child's more salient as well as subtle cues are and to spot moments where the adult responded or interjected comments in synchrony with the child's tempo and focus.

Items #4 and 5: Appropriate Stimulation

Provides appropriate stimulation, activities, and play for the child's age and stage; encourages and facilitates child's play with objects and materials. According to Clarke-Stewart (1973), the environment most growth-facilitating will not only be warm and loving, but also will be stimulating in terms of visual, verbal, and material input. Naturally, what is appropriate will vary throughout the birth- to three-year-old age range. The point is that the caregiver needs to be aware of the child's changing needs and abilities with regard to toys, books, and activities, and needs to be providing for them.

With regard to young infants, Sugarman (1984) has observed that between about four and eight or ten months of age, the child seems to be building up a repertoire of simple unitary actions to perform on single objects [See Chapter 2, p. 22 "Signalling of Intention"]. At eight or ten months of age, coordinated object and person behaviors appear, and within a month or so, the first spontaneous words. It seems quite possible that some level of object manipulation and play is very important for the infant's communication development. Consequently, in the early stages, the interventionist can encourage the parent in helping the child to build a repertoire of simple interactive games and routines with people, as well as actions with a variety of objects.

For any age child, the interventionist can demonstrate or coach the parent regarding ways in which a number of very simple everyday materials (e.g. a ball, blocks, play dough, paper) can be played with and talked about. Naturally, as the child gets older, this will include alternate and more complex ways of creatively using materials. Chapter 4 includes brief descriptions of what children are "like" at various ages. The references cited may provide additional ideas for types of games, objects, activities which are appropriate at different times.

II. Conversational Behavior

Items in this section relate to what the caregiver does in the course of communicative interactions with the child. This section begins with behaviors associated with responding to the child's communicative attempts. This is first for two reasons. One is because this is a research finding so frequently observed (i.e. that caregivers consistently respond to infants); the other is because it highlights once again the idea of following the child rather than imposing one's own agenda on the child. But clearly, the caregiver cannot (and would not want to) *always* follow the child and respond to him. Consequently, features of efficaciously establishing a shared focus, or initiating interactions, are next in the Checklist. The final group of items are those which apply in an overall sense, to all caregiver talk in the course of communicative interactions with their hearing-impaired child.

A. In Responding to the Child

Items #6, 7, and 8: Recognizing Cues and Responding

Recognizes child's communicative attempts; responds to child's communicative attempts; responds with a response which includes a question or comment requiring a further response from the child. In order to respond to the child (Item #6), the caregiver must be able to recognize the child's communicative behaviors as such. For the older child, these may be words, with or without gestures. For the younger child, as mentioned above, communicative behaviors may be cued by rate of body movement, orientation and/or tension of the body, facial expressions, gaze direction, gaze shifts, gestures, and vocalizations (Bates et al., 1979; Bateson, 1979; Carpenter et al., 1983; Lasky and Klopp, 1982; Scaife and Bruner, 1975).

The caregiver can respond to the child's communicative attempts in words, and/or by smiling, nodding, gesturing, moving closer (Item #7). One of the most effective ways of continuing the conversational exchange is to respond, and include a question or comment that encourages the child to respond, also (Item #8). For example, an infant might reach toward an object and look back and forth between the object and the adult. The adult's response could be to smile, move the object close to the infant, and say, "Oh you want the dolly, don't you?" The expected child response would be to take the dolly and relax body tension, perhaps put it in his or her mouth or manipulate it. For an older child, the response to the child's "uh oh!" might be the adult's visual attention, moving closer, and "What happened?" The child's expected response might be to point at an object and say, "broke" or "fell down." These conversational "turnabouts" are considered to be very powerful learning devices (Kaye and Charney, 1980, 1981. See also Chapter 2, pp. 29 and 31 "Negotiation of Meaning" and "Participation-Elicitors" for additional background information.)

In both of the above examples, the infant's behaviors would probably qualify as "communicative" and "intentional" for most researchers. However, there are a large number of behaviors which occur in normally developing children prior to eight months of age which many researchers would not consider to be "intentional"—although mothers behave as if **they** do. That is, mothers behave as if every burp and sneeze of the birth to three-month-old is communicative (Harding, 1983; Kaye and Charney, 1980; Snow, 1977; and Snow et al., 1979). Gradually, the mother's requirements become more stringent for what qualifies as intentionally communicative behaviors from the child. But the mother is very responsive, even to minimal vocalizations and rudimentary gestures from the beginning of the child's life (See Chapter 2, p. 33 "Responsiveness").

Caregivers of young hearing-impaired children may need some guidance in recognizing and effectively responding to child behaviors which are potentially communicative. Particularly with intervention which begins with children who are over the age of twelve months, caregivers tend to focus on the child's production of *words* as evidence of progress. Long before words appear, there are a multitude of potentially (and actually) communicative behaviors which the caregiver can advantageously promote.

Item #9: Imitation

Imitates child's productions. Obviously, conversation consists of more than the two people imitating each other's contributions. But imitation is a normal and probably important part of caregiver-child interaction, particularly during the first twelve months. Judiciously used, it can also be an extremely valuable intervention tool to assist parents of children throughout the birth- to three-year-old age range. In order to imitate the child, the parent is automatically required to recognize and respond to the child's cues, to follow the child's interests rather than imposing the parent's own agenda, and to sense the child's tempo. By imitating the child, the parent has an excellent chance of successfully establishing a mutual focus of attention, and of engaging in turn-taking. Furthermore, it can be playful and fun!

Item #10: Providing the Words

Provides child with the words appropriate to what he/she apparently wants to express. Providing the child with the words appropriate to what he or she apparently wants to express has some of the same benefits as imitating the child's utterance. Also similarly, it requires recognizing and interpreting the child's cues, as well as following the child's lead. Snow et al., (1984), MacNamara (1972), and Vygotsky (1978) have all viewed it as vitally important for cognitive development and language-learning that there should be a correspondence between what the adult says and the objects and events in the immediately surrounding environment. If the topic and message expressed by the adult are the child's own, the adult utterance seems likely to have even more significance and impact.

There are two dangers inherent to this activity, however. The first is that the caregiver must be a keen observer of the child's cues, and as accurate an interpreter of the child's intentions as possible. If not, and there is a mismatch between the caregiver's words and the child's real message it could be at best, meaningless, and at worst, detrimental (Duchan, 1986). The other danger to guard against is also related to the caregiver's ability to determine which of the child's behaviors are potentially communicative. Providing words to describe every gesture or sound the child makes could clearly become a mindless narration of on-going events. The idea is to focus on the times when the child is actually trying to express something, and to give him the words he would use in that situation.

Examples

Context:	The child peers over the side of the high chair, points downwards, looks sad, and vocalizes.
Adult:	"Uh-oh! The cookie fell down."
	or
Context:	The child points out of the car window and vocalizes excitedly.
Adult:	"Oh look! A great big firetruck!"

Item #11: Expansions

Expands child's productions semantically or grammatically or both. Expansions are parental responses that repeat part or all of the child's preceding utterance, and add to it either semantically or syntactically or both. They can be minimal replies which basically correct or evaluate the child's utterance, or they can be more extended expansions which provide related new ideas or information (Howe, 1981). In both of the following instances, the mother's utterances are extended expansions of the child's preceding utterances that provide the child with both a syntactic alternative and a semantic extension. (See Chapter 2, p. 31 "Participation-Elicitors" for further explanation.)

Examples

Child says:	"Broke truck"
Mother says:	"Tommy broke the truck. Too bad."
	or
Child says:	"Doggie pee pee!"
Mother says:	"Oh no! The doggie went pee pee on the floor!"

Research suggests that caregivers of hearing-impaired children tend to expand their child's utterances less frequently than caregivers of normally developing children of the same age (Cross, Nienhuys, and Morris, 1980; Nienhuys et al., 1984). In cases where this is because the child's language is much-delayed relative to his same-age peer, then this may be of less concern. That is, the child's productions may be so limited that they cannot be expanded in the usual sense. But expansions are considered to be of great importance in intervention settings since they occur with great regularity in normal caregiver talk, since they model correctly for the child how to add syntactic or semantic elements to an utterance, and since they are positively correlated with measures of language development (Barnes et al., 1983; Cross, 1977; Ellis and Wells, 1980; Furrow et al., 1979; Nelson, 1973; Nelson et al., 1973; Newport, Gleitman, and Gleitman, 1977). Interestingly, it has been shown that children are more likely to imitate expansions spontaneously than any other type of adult utterance (Folger and Chapman, 1978; Scherer and Olswang, 1984; Seitz and Stewart, 1975). This may be because an expansion is directly based on the child's utterance, and thus holds some automatic interest to him. Also, the adult expansion often only adds a moderately novel element to the original utterance, and in fact, often supplies words the child probably understands, but did not use in his original utterance. When the expanded adult's utterance also contains a "hook" intended to clarify the child's message and/or which expects a response from the child, it may be even more powerful as a conversation-promoting strategy. In the examples above, the caregiver could respond with the following expansions which also contain "hooks."

Examples

"Tommy broke the truck?"

[an expansion, also a yes/no clarification question]

   or

"The doggie went pee pee *where*?"

[an expansion, also a request for specific additional information]

The examples then become not just expanded responses, but "turnabouts" as discussed in Chapter 2, pp. 34–35 (Kaye and Charney, 1980, 1981). The benefits of these responses are that the caregiver is responding to the child, is on the child's topic, is modelling a semantically/syntactically expanded and correct version of the child's utterance, is engaged in negotiating communicative meaning, and has made an attempt to elicit continued participation from the child. And in most cases, none of this requires conscious effort beyond wanting to understand and communicate with the child!

B. In Establishing Shared Attention

Items #12 and 13: Engaging the Child

Attempts to engage child; talks about what child is experiencing, looking at, doing. Item #12 is listed separately in order to refocus attention on two important elements of interaction already mentioned above as part of other items. One element relates to the items concerning affect, similar to Item #1. Whether the caregiver does or does not occasionally attempt to engage the child in playful interaction or conversation can be a clue to the parent's level of coping and/or commitment to the process (See Chapter 6, p. 224 "The Affect Agenda"). If the caregiver does not attempt to engage the child, that could be a bit of behavioral evidence that there are problems in their affective relationship or that the parent is simply feeling too hopeless or frustrated to bother. Or, a lack of attempting to engage the child may be related to the other element upon which Item #12 is intended to refocus attention. That element is that with all the emphasis on responding to the child (Items #3, 6-11), the caregiver may begin to get the impression that one is *never* supposed to initiate interaction, only to respond to the child's apparent communicative attempts. This is simply not the case. To begin with, it is impractical in terms of the daily events occurring in the child's life: Try dressing or feeding a child in a purely responsive manner! Taken to the extreme, if the adults rarely initiate communication with the child, it could deprive the child of normal opportunities to learn to respond to others' communicative attempts (including others' interests and agendas).

That said, Item #13 is there to reiterate that any child-directed utterance is likely to be most successful at capturing and maintaining the child's attention, as well as at eliciting a response, if the adult utterance has some connection with what the child is experiencing, looking at, or doing. That is, the caregiver certainly can initiate at will and on any topic, but can expect the most rewarding child response if the parent's utterance fits in with the child's state and interests at that moment. This requires observation, sensitivity, and insight into the child's behavioral cues to his or her state and interest. Chapter 2, pp. 22 and 24 ("Joint Reference" and "Content: What Gets Talked About") provides additional information important for understanding of this item. (See Items #2, 3, and 4, also.)

Item #14 and 15: Sense Modalities

Uses voice (first) to attract child's attention to objects, events, self; uses body movement, gesture, touch appropriately in attracting child's attention to objects, events, self. Items #14 and 15 concern the caregiver's use of sense modalities in attracting the child's attention. Chapter 5 treats this matter in more detail. The items here refer to adult strategies used in the course of normal interactive events. Because spoken language is primarily an acoustic event, it can most efficaciously be learned by means of acoustic input (i.e. through listening). Thus, as part of helping the child learn to listen, the caregiver is encouraged to make initial attempts to attract the child's attention using voice alone (for example through calling the child's name). Whether or not the child responds will depend upon a number of factors. These include whether or not the adult's voice was sufficiently intense for the child to hear. This, in turn, depends upon the degree of the child's hearing loss, and whether or not the caregiver spoke close enough to the microphone on the child's aid. Another factor determining the likelihood of the child's response to voice has to do with whether or not the child has yet learned that voices can have meaning and can be rewarding to respond to (through either the ensuing adult approval or message). However, it should be mentioned that in rare cases, a child with a very profound hearing loss may never be able to respond consistently to a calling voice in spontaneous situations without forewarning.

With regard to appropriateness, one of the aspects to consider is: "To **what** does one attract the child's attention?" The intention may be to get the child to look at the adult's face. Or, it may be to get the child to attend to an object or an activity. For children whose residual hearing is being maximized, in a large proportion of situations, there may, in fact, be a preference that the child look at the objects or activity—and not at the adult's face—as the message is delivered. The words used (e.g. "Susie—look at this!") and indicating the object by moving it, touching it, or pointing to it are all commonly used ways of attracting the child's attention away from the face. Another strategy is to have the object near the face as the name is called, and to move it away as soon as the child turns to look. Often, the child's gaze will follow the moving object as the rest of the message is said.

In most normal interactive situations, attracting the child's attention using voice alone is probably unproductive beyond about three attempts. At that point, it can be assumed that the child has simply not heard, or is too engrossed in something else to listen to a relatively faint auditory signal, or has not learned the meaning behind being called, or has decided that it is more rewarding **not** to attend than to attend! Calling a child seven or eight times in a row can be a frustrating and disheartening experience for the caller—and it may even inadvertently be teaching the child not to respond until the eighth (very loud and exasperated) time.

Other attention-attracting strategies to use after the auditory ones include attempting to attract the child's visual attention by leaning forward or gesturing within his visual field, or by drawing a toy across the child's visual field to the speaker's face (assuming attention to the face is desired) or to some other position (perhaps a table with other toys) as the rest of the message is said. Tapping the child to attract his attention is obviously also possible, as well as less subtle.

C. In General

Item #16: Sentence Complexity

Uses phrases and sentences of appropriate length and complexity. This item needs to be interpreted with caution and some latitude. Research fairly consistently reports that adults use sentences of approximately eight morphemes when speaking with each other, and of about three to five morphemes when speaking with children from birth through toddlerhood (Phillips, 1973; Stern et al., 1983). However research results are markedly inconsistent [see Snow et al., 1987, for a review] regarding the exact nature of the semantic/syntactic changes which occur, and when and why they occur during the birth-to three-year-old age period. For example, with very young infants (i.e. birth to two months), some mothers use utterances of adult length as they croon and talk to them. Then, perhaps as the child shows an increasing capability of participating in face-to-face play interactions, some mothers reduce the length and complexity of their utterances to fit more closely with the child's early smiling and babbling exchanges. Other mothers use short utterances from the beginning. And after the child begins using words, some mothers match the child's utterance length, while some stay several morphemes in advance.

Lacking whatever certainty research could provide for this item, the interventionist can rely on what seems sensible from a communication and learning point of view. An argument could be made that if an adult is using very long and complex sentences with a young child, it is possible that the adult has no expectation that the child will understand what is being said. With the neonate, the mother's long crooning sentences are likely to be more a part of the mother's efforts to provide a safe and comforting environment for the child, than a part of attempting to communicate specific messages to the child. When an adult uses very long sentences with an older child, it can sometimes actually sound as if the adult is talking to himself or herself, rather than to the child. In intervention settings, the intent generally **is** to communicate with the child. One is striving for the child's understanding. Consequently, the three-to-five morpheme length is probably a reasonable guideline for most caregiver utterances.

As for whether the caregiver's utterances should match or stay slightly in advance of the child's utterance length, it seems likely that the caregiver's utterance length and complexity will generally be a bit in advance of the child. Certainly, this will automatically be the case if the caregiver is speaking primarily in phrases and sentences (rather than in single words) in order to provide more complete "acoustic envelopes," and if the caregiver is responding to the child's utterances using expansions and/or turnabouts [see Chapter 5; Also Item #11].

Items #17, 18, 19, 20: Manner of Speaking

Pauses expectantly after speaking to encourage child to respond; speaks to child with appropriate rate, intensity, and pitch; uses interesting, animated voice; uses normal, unexaggerated mouth movements. All of these items (#17, 18, 19, 20) relate to the manner in which the caregiver delivers the message to the child. They are interrelated, but it is possible for one item to be problematic and not the others.

Pausing after speaking to encourage the child to respond (Item #17) is a fundamental part of turn-taking. In practice, it can mean giving the child the space (time) to "get a word in edgewise," or it can mean waiting long enough for the child to process the adult message and to respond to it. According to Stern, et al (1983), maternal pausing between utterances is greatest at birth and declines somewhat after basic turn-taking rules are established. However, between-utterance pauses even at two years of age are still approximately twice as long as they are in Adult-Adult utterances.

The caregiver's rate of speaking (Item #18) also tends to be a bit slower in Adult-Child speech than in Adult-Adult speech, with enunciation somewhat clearer. Clarifying the message in these ways could be important in many instances as an aid to the child's understanding. But it would be most reasonable to maintain a normal rate of about three-to-five syllables per second (Ling, 1976) in order to avoid distorting the message. At slower rates, there can be a tendency to over-enunciate: to mouth the articulatory movements to an excessive extent. And this can create a situation where the child can only understand people who make exaggerated mouth movements. (Not surprisingly, these are also often the *children* who overexaggerate.) If the rate is careful-but-normal, the mouth movements are also likely to be normal and unexaggerated (Item #20).

Intensity (Item #18) should be normal (not shouting and not murmuring) in order to avoid inadvertently distorting the acoustic signal, and must take into account the child's hearing range (Ling, 1981). The closer the speaker's mouth is to the child's hearing aid microphone, the louder it will be for the child. The generally accepted optimal distance is four to six inches from the microphone. However, in normal conversational situations the optimum speaking distance is entirely dependent upon the degree of the child's hearing loss, the level of background noise, the social context, and the presence or absence of FM devices.

In normal motherese, the overall pitch is generally higher and the intonational contours more varied than in Adult-Adult talk. If the overall pitch is too high (Item #18), it may give a less-than-optimal signal to a child with a high frequency hearing loss. However, varied intonational contours and an interesting, animated voice (Item #19) are likely to be well within the hearing capabilities of nearly all hearing-impaired children. Since these voice features are used to get and maintain the child's attention (Stern et al., 1983), as well as to cue constituent boundaries, sentence types, and speech acts, it is especially important that caregivers incorporate them when talking to hearing-impaired children.

Items #21 and 22: Sense Modalities Again

Uses audition-maximizing techniques; uses appropriate gesture. Items #21 and 22 concern the caregiver's use of sense modalities in situations other than attracting the child's attention (see Items #14 and 15). The principles are the same, in that auditory input is the preferred choice for presenting an acoustically based communication modality (i.e. spoken language). Techniques for maximizing the child's audition include speaking well within the child's hearing range; using a normal overall pitch and rate of speaking; using an animated, interesting voice with varied intonational contours; speaking while sitting behind or beside the child; obscuring the child's view of the lips using the hand or a piece of paper; and attracting the child's visual focus away from the face and to the toys or activities at hand while speaking. Depending upon the degree of the child's hearing loss and familiarity with the task, some of the auditory-only input may be quickly followed by or alternated with additional access to visual input (e.g. looking at the face). Visual and tactile modalities will need to be employed as the more severe degrees of hearing loss necessitate it. The interventionist's knowledge of the acoustic correlates of speech sounds, as well as of the individual child's audiogram are essential to determining appropriate and realistically high expectations.

The amount of gesture that is appropriate (Item #22) is another item having to be interpreted with some flexibility according to the individual case and contexts. Research suggests that gestures are essential in the child's early communicative attempts (Bates et al., 1979). In fact, most child communications include gestures throughout the birth- to three-year-old time period (Carpenter et al., 1983; Lasky and Klopp, 1982). So it would be understandable if caregivers were also using gestures fairly extensively at this time. This area needs further research. However, the item has been included on the Checklist, to allow focus and discussion of this area in situations where the amount of parental gesture seems excessive. It seems logical that it would be detrimental to the child's concentration on the spoken language part of the message (the acoustic input) if most of the message is also conveyed through gesture (visual input). This notion also merits further research investigation, however, as it is one of the fundamental points of contention in the on-going "Oral-Total Communication" debate.

4

Clusters of Child Achievements

What we have to learn to do, we learn by doing.
(Aristotle, 384-322 B.C.)

This chapter discusses clusters of achievements in the areas of communication, language, and speech which are accomplished by normally developing children from birth to three years of age. Some early-detected hearing-impaired children with appropriate hearing aids and input can be expected to exhibit this sequence of achievements within the same age range as their normally hearing peers. Others may not demonstrate the same abilities at the same time as their normally hearing peers, but they can be expected and encouraged to follow the same general sequence. A few others, even with great commitment on the part of all involved, may not follow a normal developmental pattern leading towards the acquisition of spoken language. This becomes enormously important information for professionals and parents as they attempt to evaluate whether or not the approaches being used are appropriate. Wisely used, the kind of developmental information offered here can be invaluable in assessing a child's general developmental level, in charting progress, in planning instructional events, and in predicting and promoting the accomplishments to come. For this discussion, the birth- to three-year-old age period is divided into the following stages which are each addressed in turn:

Becoming communicative: (birth to six months of age)

Understanding more and more: (six–twelve months of age)

Saying some words: (twelve–eighteen months of age)

Connecting words in phrases: (eighteen–twenty-four months of age)

Increasing the complexity: (twenty-four–thirty-six months of age)

A stage model has been used for this discussion as a convenience for managing the vast amount of learning and change which occur in children between birth and age three. However, an individual child's progress does not trace such an orderly, hierarchical sequence as might be implied from the use of stages to describe the changes and accomplishments. Individual children take numerous routes in the journey toward communicative competency, many of which the developmental map-making scholars and researchers have not yet fully charted. Some of this variety in developmental routes and rates is related to differences in personalities, learning styles, usage of available sense modalities, and the amount and nature of exposure to and involvement in fluent communication. Nonetheless, there is a general progression from knowing and doing less, to knowing and doing more. That general progression is what is described here.

The validity of any scholarly description of development depends upon the characteristics of the subjects in the research upon which the description is based. To date, the vast majority of normal developmental studies have had middle-class mainstream North American children as subjects. The description here is thus a presentation of major themes regarding the communication, language, and speech accomplishments of the birth to three-year-old age period as they have been observed to occur in the research on middle-class mainstream North American children.

Each stage will begin with a brief description of general behavioral characteristics of children of that particular age and stage (*What the Child Is Like*). Generalizing about behavior in this manner is, of course, risky since babies are such incredibly complex individuals from birth.

Furthermore, the range of what is normal is enormous. Gersh (1966) describes a ten-year study which identified a number of dimensions upon which normally developing children vary widely. An individual child's characteristic behaviors for each of these dimensions appeared in early infancy and remained constant to later childhood. The dimensions were activity level, regularity/predictability, adaptability to change in routine, level of sensory threshold, overall mood, intensity of response to stimuli, distractibility, and persistence. The totality of the child's characteristic behaviors on these dimensions seems to have much to do with descriptions of his or her personality or temperament. Brazelton (1983) addresses these differences with stage-by-stage descriptions of three types of baby personalities: active, average, and quiet. He says that an individual baby is likely to be more like one of the types than the other, but that any baby will exhibit characteristics of any of the three types at various moments. An interesting additional observation by Ames, Ilg, and Haber (1982a, b) of the Gesell Institute of Child Development is that the development of emotional behavior in infancy and early childhood is marked by alternating periods of equilibrium and disequilibrium. The equilibrium tends to reach a pinnacle at the year points, and disequilibrium at the half-year points. So, for example, age two is peaceful, age two and a half is chaotic. Their contention is that the state of equilibrium seems to need to break up in order to allow the child to reorganize into a higher state of equilibrium. The changes seem to be internal to the child, although the child's behavior can be improved or made worse by the environment.

In any case, the descriptions here are not intended to be great academic treatises, but simple, rough guidelines to provide a bit of context for the descriptions of communicative accomplishments which follow. They are based on a composite of information from Ames and Ilg, 1976; Ames, Ilg, and Haber, 1982a, 1982b; Brazelton, 1983; Cryer, Helms, and Bouland, 1988; Glover, Preminger, and Sanford, 1978; Missouri Dept. of Elementary and Secondary Education, 1982; Leach, 1976; Schwartz and Miller, 1988; Spock and Rothenberg, 1985; and, White, 1985.

After each section describing the child's overall behavior at a particular age/stage, is a section detailing the child's communication and language achievements during that same time. The third and final section for each stage describes vocalization and/or speech development. The intention throughout the chapter is to preserve the interwoven complexity of the learning, while clearly demonstrating progressive acquisition of knowledge and abilities from one stage to the next.

Becoming Communicative: (Birth to Six Months)

What the Child Is Like

A long-standing child development adage says that infants develop from head to toe. That is, they first learn about the world through their eyes, ears, and mouth. This learning is in the form of looking about almost continuously when awake, responding to some noises, and putting nearly all available objects in the mouth. Newborn infants' primary interests are in feeding, being clean, and feeling comfortable and secure. From birth to six months, infants are increasingly active, awake, and sociable.

By six months of age, infants can sit with support and hold up their heads, which increases their access to visual stimulation. They look directly at faces, recognize their mothers, and smile and vocalize when paid attention to. Six-month-old babies can reach for, pick up, and grasp objects. This means that they can feed themselves crackers, hold their own bottles, and may pick up their spoons and mess about with them. This also means that they can pick up toys; sometimes they fuss if a favorite toy is removed from their grasp. Six-month-olds can anticipate events such as feeding, and the mother's face re-appearing in Peek-a-Boo games. They show an awareness of routines, and attempt to make enjoyable sensations or events recur.

Communication and Language Developments

It is during this earliest period of development that infants begin to learn about conversations. Indeed, infants do learn *how* to converse before they are able to use any formal language system. (See also the section in Chapter 2, pp. 18–24, "Child's Development of Interactional Abilities.")

During pregnancy, parents imagine how their child will look and how he or she will act. They expect that the child will be "normal" which encompasses the idea that their child will learn to talk and use language. When the child is finally born, parents immediately begin to treat the infant as if he or she could communicate. Of course, parents know that a newborn cannot understand what is said nor produce meaningful language. Nevertheless, most parents interact with their infant as if they could participate in conversations. Even when very young infants vocalize or seem to be aware of the environment, parents respond to these behaviors as if they were communicative efforts (Golinkoff, 1983; Miller, 1988), as the following example illustrates:

> Adrienne is cuddled next to her mother. She looks at a nearby baby bottle, turns her head, waits a few seconds, arches her back, and says, "ghhhh!"

> Mother responds by saying, "Oh, do you want something to eat? The bottle's empty! Do you want something to eat?"

Parents who make the assumption that their infant has potential for communication, are extremely attentive to any apparent communicative attempts—whether they be vocalizations, gestures and pointing, or even eye contact or gazing. This vigilance on the part of parents is quite critical to subsequent communication/language development, for it aids in the forging of an emotional bond between infant and parent, a platform upon which subsequent communication development is constructed.

Up to about two to three months of age, much of the "talk" that occurs between parents and infants is overlapping or occurs at the same time (Ginsburg and Kilbourne, 1988). The infant starts to vocalize, and the caregiver (mother) reflects back an interpretation of what the infant appears to be "saying." At four to six months of age, interactions change from overlapping to turn-taking. Responsibility for this change lies initially with the parents, who begin to time their talk to follow or precede their infant's vocalizing, even when the infant doesn't appear to be interested in interacting. That is, parents may deliberately attempt to provoke communicative behavior in the infant to begin or prolong interaction (Kaye and Wells, 1980). For example, let's imagine a mother holding her four-month-old. At first, the baby vocalizes and the mother responds, but then the baby does not continue the "conversation" for some reason. The mother may jiggle the baby to provoke additional attention or vocalization. If successful, the conversation will continue; if not, the conversation will terminate. This switch in focus from overlapped to turn-taking interactions is important since conversation in most languages is based on one person talking at a time (Sacks, Schlegloff, and Jefferson, 1974). Thus, the roots of conversation can be observed even at these very young ages.

Another aspect of conversation learned during this age period is the expectation that participants will converse on mutually agreeable topics, that are known to both partners. In the birth- to six-month period, topics are usually established by the infant, except in those situations involving necessary everyday life routines such as changing diapers, feeding, or getting ready for bed (Gleitman, Newport, and Gleitman, 1984; Snow, Perlman, and Nathan, 1987). Initially, topics are determined by the infant's gaze. If a child looks at the mother's braid swinging next to her face, the mother will probably initiate a conversation about the braid. As the infant gains motor control, topics are determined not only by gaze, but by actions such as attempts to grasp an object or to more toward a person or toy. The caregiver may also attempt to introduce topics by moving objects within the infant's field of gaze or reach. Whether this succeeds in eliciting a response depends entirely on the infant. If he or she doesn't respond by attending to the person or object, the caregiver usually does not pursue that agenda, unless it is required for completing a necessary routine such as feeding.

Throughout this birth- to six-month age period, interactions become longer and longer. In some cases, they are formalized into games, such as Peek-a-Boo, Where's-the-Doggy, Patty-Cake, or other family favorites (Bruner, 1981). These routines or games appear to be another important element in subsequent language development. They serve as scaffolds for the early introduction of language. If a father and daughter consistently engage in a particular form of the Peek-a-Boo game, it becomes predictable or familiar. This allows the parent to change any language he uses in the routine, while knowing that the interaction will be successful since he can depend on the fact that his daughter knows how the game is played. In this way, the format is held constant, while the language can be varied. This allows the infant to concentrate his or her attention on the new language, rather than being confused by a new format **and** new language simultaneously. Part of what is being modeled in games or routines is the idea that conversations include comments that are appropriate to the topic at hand. That is, parents are showing the infant that talk needs to be relevant. This idea becomes increasingly important as the infant's language comprehension abilities develop, in part as an outgrowth of these games and routines.

Although there is no formal linguistic expression observed during this period of development, there is evidence suggesting that the child may be developing some understanding that speech can be used as communicative behavior (Bloom, Russell, and Wassenberg, 1987; Delack, 1978). When an adult engages in turn-taking with a three-month-old infant, the infant usually produces a higher rate of "speech-like" vocalizations. It has also been shown that by three months of age, infants produce different vocalizations in different communication situations such as self-initiated "happy" sounds in pleasant situations, and self-initiated "sad" sounds in unpleasant situations. Indeed, there is a significant correlation between the extent of an infant's differential vocal productions at three months of age and performance on a variety of tests of linguistic functioning at twelve years of age (Roe, McClure, and Roe, 1982). Generating different vocalizations in different social situations is clearly an important step toward expression of a variety of communication purposes.

In summary, then, the period between birth to six months involves the development of a growing sense of communication. The child is exposed to the processes of establishing and maintaining topics, and to taking turns that are appropriately timed and relevant to the established topic. Through vocalizations, the infant also exhibits a growing understanding of the idea that one communicates differently in different communication situations.

Vocalization and Speech Developments

Much of the vocalizing an infant does during this period is in direct response to stimulation, and is referred to as "reflexive" (Stark, 1978, 1980). This includes crying from hunger or discomfort, grunts, sighs, and feeding noises. However, there are some nonreflexive vocalizations produced by the infant even in the first month of life. These "speechy" vocalizations are the ones of interest here, as they increase in frequency, complexity, and "speechiness" across the first year. Oller (1977, 1980, 1983) has proposed that the sequence of vocalization development in the first year reflects an increasing capacity to manipulate a set of general, universal characteristics underlying adult phonologies. Oller uses the term "metaphonological" for these background parameters, which include both suprasegmental and segmental capabilities. In the first month of life, the infant's nonreflexive vocalizations are called "Quasi-Resonated Nuclei" (QRN's). These vocalizations are characterized by normal phonation (in that they are not excessively breathy or strident), but spectrographic analysis reveals that they lack full adult-like resonances—hence the term, quasi-re-sonated. QRN's can range in sound from a syllabic nasal consonant-like production to a high, mid, unrounded vowel-like production with much nasal emission. They can be produced with the mouth closed, or nearly so. This early phonating is considered to be the most basic of the metaphonological capabilities which the child develops in the first year.

During months two and three, the child's vocalizations continue to be primarily reflexive. In addition, the vast majority (roughly 75 percent according to Oller, 1977) of the infant's nonreflexive vocalizations continue to be QRN's. However, a new element begins to appear with some frequency in the infant's nonreflexive vocalizations: the GOO. This is a QRN, often sounding like a rounded back vowel such as /u/, in combination with a velar or uvular closure. This stage is sometimes referred to as the "Cooing" stage. These combinations can have either CV or VC shapes (using C and V loosely), and they can occur in isolation or repetitively. Syllabification at this stage is primitive (Zlatin and Horii, 1976), in that the timing of the transitions is often considerably longer than the adult model. However, the appearance of GOO's does indicate that the child is developing a capacity to produce a rudimentary opposition between closure and opening of the vocal tract. These are considered to be an important metaphon-ological achievement as they provide the first evidence of consonant-like oppositions.

Oller refers to months four, five, and six as the "Expansion Stage" in vocalization development (1977, 1980, 1983). It is during this time that the child seems to explore the capacities of the vocal mechanism. Now the vowels are more fully resonated, and more and more of the productions are combinations of vowels with consonant-like elements. The emergence of fully resonated phonation allows the child to more fully exploit the resonance capabilities of the vocal tract. Resonance patterns can now be more widely varied. Since all languages system-atically manipulate contrasts of resonance in vowel productions, this is considered to mark the emergence of another important meta-phonological feature: the underlying capacity for vowel differentia-tion. Studies have shown that the vowels most often perceived by listeners include /ɛ, I, æ, ∧, ʊ/, although /ɛ/ is by far the most frequent (33 percent of all vowels heard). The back-rounded vowels /o/ and

/u/ were the least frequently perceived at about 1 percent each (Lieberman, 1980).

A number of other new elements also emerge during the expansion stage (Oller, 1977, 1980, 1983; Stark, 1978, 1980). Squealing and growling are two of these elements. Squealing productions usually either begin or end in a normal pitch register, but also include a highly tense maximal fundamental frequency, a falsetto pitch, often above 500 Hz. Growling, on the other hand, has a much lower fundamental frequency (150 Hz or below), and may be characterized by tense, "creaky" voicing. Squeals and growls are thus considered to represent the infant's developing capacity to manipulate the metaphonological parameters of pitch contrast and vocal quality (Oller, 1977, 1980, 1983).

Yelling is another feature of vocal behavior from four to six months of age. The occurrence of yells may indicate the child's developing metaphonological ability to manipulate amplitude variations. This ability will later be important for prosodic (e.g. stress) and paralinguistic (e.g. emotive) purposes.

"Raspberries" (bilabial or labiolingual trills) also appear from four to six months of age. This is considered to mark a beginning capacity to manipulate the place of articulatory closure.

Near the end of the expansion stage, another category called "Marginal Babbling" emerges, although not with great frequency of occurrence. This is when the child produces combinations of consonant-like and vowel-like elements, which still do not exhibit mature transitional timing characteristics. In marginal babbling, the transitions are frequently very slow (greater than one hundred milliseconds) and shaky, rather than smooth. This can be considered to be a maturing of the primitive alternations of open and closed vocal tract seen at two to three months in the Cooing Stage.

Understanding More and More: (Six–Twelve Months)

What the Child Is Like

During this stage, infants tend to be friendly, curious, and affectionate. They grow to enjoy face-to-face interactive games such as Pattycake,

Hide-and-Seek, Round and Round the Garden, and This Little Piggy Went to Market. They will repeat a performance when laughed at; they love and encourage an audience. Across this time period, infants progress from sitting to creeping, to crawling, to standing, and sometimes to walking. Their balance is not great, their memories short, and they have no sense of danger—all of which conspires to require that their living spaces must be conscientiously child-proofed.

At this age, infants spend a fair amount of time visually inspecting objects, and doing things with them such as banging them together, dropping them (repeatedly if someone picks them up in-between), throwing them, taking them apart, putting smaller objects into big ones, turning wheels. They also like to manipulate simple mechanical devices such as light switches and pop-up toys. Six- to twelve-month-olds can find a block hidden under a cup right in front of them, can pull on a string to obtain a toy, and will squeeze a toy to make it squeak or move in some way. They will often imitate gestures such as clapping or waving "bye-bye," as well as speech and animal sounds.

At the same time, infants between six and twelve months may be beginning to assert themselves by demanding attention, insisting on holding their own bottles, showing impatience at being cuddled, avoiding having their faces washed, and pushing others away in order to keep toys with which they are playing.

Communication and Language Developments

This period involves the continued growth of understanding about communication. It is also the period when children begin to evidence specific understanding of aspects of the language addressed to them. Although use of real words is not present during this period for every child, utterances of normally developing infants show clear evidence of social uses for their vocalizations.

By ten months of age, communicative interactions are organized in such a way that they follow the turn-taking rules of English almost exactly (Freedle and Lewis, 1977). Such interactions have been called proto-conversations. During these conversations, infants tend to wait for caretakers to complete their talk, while caretakers tend to do the same for their infants. There is virtually no overlapping communication behavior, except for appropriate acts such as laughing together, singing songs, or the instances of mother talking to prevent the child from hurting him/herself. Qualitatively, however, the nature of interactions changes during this period of time. At three months of age, mothers accept almost any vocalization as communicative (Snow, 1977). By seven months of age, however, mothers prefer more "speech-like" utterances. For instance, following a particular infant production, the mother might be observed to say, "No, I didn't say that! I said '_____.' " The mother might then model a more speech-like, multiple syllable production. Or, the mother might say, "What's that?" followed by an expectant look cueing the child to try again. Over the first few years of life, parents consistently increase their expectations about the length and complexity of their children's utterances. It is important to understand, however, that this type of encouragement toward length and complexity normally never dominates interactions between parents and their children. If it did, then the children would probably soon be reluctant to converse with adults.

During this period, the role of games and routines continues to expand, with an important change noted. The parent now attempts to exchange roles with the infant (Bruner, 1981). For example, at some point in the game, the mother hands the handkerchief used in a Peek-a-Boo game to the infant and says, *You* hide." This provides the infant with an excellent opportunity to learn and use the language appropriate to this familiar and highly motivating game. The mother only initiates role changes, however, when she feels that her infant clearly understands how the game is played and what he or she is supposed to do.

Six to twelve months is also the period when the infant begins to attend to specific aspects of language itself. That is, infants begin to understand what is said to them. Obviously, we know much less about how infants learn to understand language than we do about how they use language. We can hear and record what young children say, but it is very difficult to ask a ten-month-old exactly what he or she understands. In spite of these limitations, recent research does allow us to gain some insight into the early comprehension abilities of children.

We know that children's understanding of language exceeds their production of language (Benedict, 1979). Young children understand their first words earlier than they produce their first words. Indeed, many children acquire an understanding of the first fifty words before production mastery of the first five or six. Interestingly, the first words understood by children are not necessarily the first words produced by those same children. In other words, the order of acquisition of words comprehended is not matched by the order of acquisition of words produced.

Comprehension of words in a particular situation seems to be related to the context in which they are uttered. Interestingly, infants appear to attend first to words that, to an adult, may seem to be less obvious in the communication situation. For example, if an infant is handed a ball by the parent with the injunction, "Throw the ball," he does not have to understand the word *ball*. It is self-evident what object the mother is talking about since she has just handed the ball to the child. What the infant has to understand is *throw* since throwing is less contextually clear. In contrast, if the mother and child are playing with a set of zoo animals and the mother points toward the toy box and says, "Get me the elephant," it is the word *elephant* that the child must understand, for the point coupled with the play context clearly indicates that something particular is being requested. Comprehension of specific words is a reason to attend to those specific words. The reason may also be related to aspects of events which the child enjoys. For example, the child may quickly come to understand "Up?" in connection with getting picked up and cuddled, or "More?" in connection with eating favorite foods. Obviously, the words first comprehended by infants represent a variety of form categories, not just nouns, but verbs, adjectives, and prepositions as well.

Investigations of the meaning assigned by very young children to words suggest that those meanings may be narrower or more diffuse in meaning than they are for adults (Barrett, 1986; Bowerman, 1978). For some children, a common word may refer only to a specific object, a specific action, or a specific location. *Doggy* may refer just to the family pet; the word *up* may only be understood when Daddy reaches down toward the child; *in* may only be understood in reference to putting toys in a box, but not a bag. For the same children, some words may refer to a global concept that contains undifferentiated elements of subjectness, of emotion, or of personal experience. It is important to know that young children may understand words differently from adults, and that this difference in understanding may be an essential initial stepping stone.

In addition to growth in comprehension during the six-to twelve-month stage, infants use vocalizations which are increasingly varied and communicative in nature. From six months to the appearance of the first word, the infant extends both vocal and gestural behavior to include deliberate acts of communication that initiate interactions with others. These intentional acts normally include both eye and hand gestures, pointing, and vocalizations. What makes pointing communicative and intentional? If the infant is observed to attempt to make eye contact with a partner while gesturing or vocalizing, communication has been initiated. Infants often alternate gaze between an object of interest and the communication partner. This latter act seems particularly important since it sends a precise message that the partner should attend to a specific topic. This action is referred to as a "communicative point." Eye contact is generally recognized as an important signal to the conversational partner that the vocalizations and gestures used by the infant are communicative (Bates, 1979; Bates, Shore, Bretherton, and McNew, 1983). The infant may also be observed to wait for a response from the communication partner. If these gestures and vocalizations are not intentional, if they are not communicative, then why do infants wait for a response from others? Infants of this age will also persist in trying to establish a topic until parents or caregivers provide a response. Persistence also suggests that vocalizations and gestures are important elements of communication for infants.

Over time, some gesture/vocalization combinations evolve into communicative routines. For example, the infant may consistently reach for an object and say "uh" when he wants it. This kind of routine is referred to as a proto-communication form (Bates, 1979; Blake and Fink, 1987; Carter, 1979). Investigation of these early proto-types indicate that they tend to serve three important functions, namely, to regulate the other's behavior, to establish social interaction, and to sustain joint attention on topics. For example, the infant who kicks his high chair and vocalizes "mmm" while looking at mother is using a proto-form to establish social interaction in the form of attracting her attention. At some point after obtaining the mother's attention, the child points toward a cookie on the counter and says, "Da." The mother turns to look at the cookie, and says, "Oh, you found a cookie!" The child's proto-form behavior has thus initiated the establishment of joint attention toward the cookie. If the child then leans towards the cookie as he is pointing to it, says "Da!" more forcefully, and kicks his chair, the mother may then know that he wants her to give him the cookie. He has thus regulated her behavior in enlisting her help to achieve his goal. The nature and types of proto-forms developed by an infant are dependent upon his or her particular communicative environment. The child will only develop proto-forms for those situations in which he has a need and an opportunity to communicate. The richer the communicative environment, the richer the proto-forms developed by the child.

Initially, the vocal component of proto-forms consists of consistent syllables such as *wa, nnn, mmm,* or *da.* These are called "vocables" and seem to represent the child's first attempts to produce word-like utterances (Ferguson, 1978). It is important to realize that these productions, while not real words, are complements to gestures. The communicative attempt is comprised of the whole complex of vocalization, gesture, and gaze. As the infant progresses toward age one, the single sounds are replaced by more word-like utterances. For instance, these early efforts may be treated by parents as real words, they are more properly regarded as communication acts which cannot be meaningfully separated from the gestures and specific communication situations in which they consistently occur. Although proto-forms and vocables are not real words, they should be recognized as another important step toward spoken language acquisition.

In summary, the period from six to twelve months involves the continued development of a sense of communication. The child's ability to initiate and sustain conversation on specific topics continues to grow. In addition, the child begins to evidence growth in understanding of language. Understanding of language precedes the production of language, but there is not a direct parallel between the order in which words are understood and which they are produced. Which words a particular child chooses to learn depends upon his communication needs and the types of communication situations to which he has been exposed. Although there is no development of formal productive language, the child does begin to develop proto-forms that include both oral (vocables) and non-oral components. These proto-forms are seen as immediate precursors to the development of spoken language.

Vocalization and Speech Developments

During this time period the timing of the consonant-vowel transitions becomes more consistent with the timing in adult speech (i.e. from thirty to seventy-five milliseconds). This achievement of genuine syllabic productions marks the onset of "Canonical" or "Reduplicated" babbling (Oller, 1977, 1980, 1983; Stark, 1978, 1980). These are the /bababa/ or /dadada/ sequences, which parents often recognize as a developmental milestone. It should be noted, however, that between seven to ten months, at least half of the vocal behaviors are vocalizations which are *not* reduplicated. By about eleven to twelve months of age, the infant's vocal behaviors are dominated by multi-syllabic sequences, which often contain varied consonants and vowels within a single vocalized unit (e.g. /bada/ or /wiwa/). This behavior is called "Variegated Babbling," and it often sounds as if the child is talking since it contains intonation and stress marking. This variegated babbling period has been described as a phonetic "springboard" to speech (Elbers, 1982, p.45). In terms of the types of consonants used, stops and nasals predominate, with most other sounds occurring with markedly less frequency. This appears to be the case across languages (Locke, 1983). Variety in the vowel repertoire is reported to be relatively stable from six to twelve months. Lax central vowels predominate, such as /ɛ, I, æ, ʌ, ʊ/ (Lieberman, 1980).

The reader is referred to Proctor (1989) for an excellent checklist of vocal behaviors of infants from birth through twelve months of age.

Saying Some Words: (Twelve–Eighteen Months)

What the Child Is Like

Toddlers between twelve and eighteen months of age are generally eager, and exhibit something like a passion for exploring everything. They are increasingly mobile and can walk (including sideways and backwards), climb, bounce, and chase things with more and more speed. They can walk upstairs holding on, and throw or kick a large ball. They will play by themselves for ten minutes or more and enjoy activities such as pouring, emptying and filling containers, knocking down block towers, and turning pages of a book. Children at this age will draw with a crayon and try to feed themselves, although both activities require adult assistance. The beginnings of independence and negativity noted at the previous stage continue during this one.

Communication and Language Developments

Near the end of the first year of life, infants comprehend a great deal of what familiar people say to them. They also are likely to produce their first word(s), which for most parents is an enormously important event.

As we have noted, children have already learned a great deal about conversation, such as the basic rules of turn-taking, the importance of establishing a mutual topic, and the need to make meaningful on-topic contributions. Now the child begins to use spoken as well as nonverbal acts for establishing topics. Instead of merely pointing to an object, the child can now say the word to focus the adult's attention. Early productive abilities are quite limited, of course, and are used primarily to mark the most critical aspects of the situation. That is, first words are generally used to make comments rather than to topicalize (Greenfield, Reilly, Leaper, and Baker, 1985). If a child can only say single words, it is probably more efficient communicatively for him to point to a large toy horse in a grocery store and use his one word to say "up" (rather than to say "horse").

During this twelve- to eighteen-month period, parents and children engage in extended play sequences. Building block houses, playing with toy animals, or feeding the dolly become more prominent as the focus of adult-child interactions. First words are often used to mark these social events. Children use first words to indicate when an act is completed, when an act has failed, or when they want an act to be repeated. Gopnik (1988) reported on twelve- to eighteen-month-old children who showed completion of difficult tasks by uttering "dere" to signal success. Failures were indicated by "oh, dear," while "more" signalled a desire to repeat a task. These utterances should be recognized as social regulators, rather than words that are intended only to convey lexical meaning.

At around one year of age, parents begin to make their children aware of the need to greet (say "hi"), to terminate conversations (bye-bye), to express politeness (thank-you), and to demonstrate social awareness (Happy Birthday!, Trick or Treat!) (Gleason, Perlman, and Grief, 1984). Use of these forms should be seen primarily as a means of regulating social interactions since twelve-month-olds will certainly not have grasped the concept of being polite.

Previously, we indicated that the earliest words understood by children may have very narrow or very broad meanings. During this period, as well as in subsequent stages, children further refine their understanding of the meanings of words. A child can be said to understand a word when he recognizes that it stands for a class of objects or events that share common characteristics. Research suggests that when children acquire a new word, it tends to have a fairly restricted meaning (Kuczaj, 1986; Lucariello, 1987; Mervis and Crisalfi, 1982). For instance, the word *birdie* may initially mean only the family pet, but eventually, it will be extended to include other birds that look only vaguely alike, but may not include extremes such as ostriches, hummingbirds, or penguins. The initial restriction in the child's understanding of the meaning is called "underextension." The boundaries of the word's meaning expand as the child has more experiences with it. Indeed, the number of words the child acquires and the breadth of each word's meaning depends entirely on the extent of each child's experience with words (Adams and Bullock, 1986; Banigan and Mervis, 1989; Mervis and Mervis, 1982, 1988). If parents restrict the topics they share with a child, the number of word experiences available to the child will be limited. If the parent uses particular words only in limited situations, then the breadth of the meaning categories the child develops will be restricted as well. To some extent, both types of restrictions are part of most children's experience. The restrictions may even be helpful for establishing an initial understanding of a particular word. The point simply is that if meaning categories have been initially restricted, it should not be surprising when children of this age demonstrate knowledge of only those restricted meanings.

During the twelve- to eighteen-month period children also begin to pay attention to whole sentences as well as single words. Indeed, children apparently can understand whole sentences long before they can produce them. That is, young children may understand the word order constraints of English well before eighteen months of age while they are not likely to produce multiple word utterances until after that age (Pinker, 1984).

As mentioned previously, during the twelve- to eighteen-month stage most children first produce single words. Words are "real" when they can be separated from specific communication situations. That is, the word has to be used in more than one communicative situation, and has to be used independent of any gestural support. Examination of the earliest words produced by children shows that words fall into a number of categories, namely: general nouns *doggy*, specific nouns *mommy*, action words *up*, *eat*, modifiers *dirty*, *nice*, and personal-social words *want*, *please* (Benedict, 1979). Most general nouns tend to represent objects that the child can act on such as food, toys, and articles of clothing rather than immovable objects such as table, floor, or window. Some children tend to focus initially on general nouns, while others tend to focus their attention on social/emotional words (Lieven, 1980; Nelson, 1973). Despite these early differences, both groups of children become competent language users.

When children use early words, they tend to signal certain aspects of meaning. Children are anxious to talk about who (agent) is doing what (action) to whom (patient) in what place (location) (Edwards and Goodwin, 1986). Young children are also interested in talking about the state of objects, characteristics of objects and events, as well as who owns what. This results in the use of words to signal that something is located in a box *there*, to signal a ball's color *red*, or to signal who owns a particular pair of shoes *mommy*. When children use words to encode any of the above categories, they are using words with particular lexical meaning. At other times, however, these same words can function as social regulators. The following is an example of this change in focus:

> Benjamin excitedly says, "Doggy! Doggy! Doggy!" jumping up and down, and looking back and forth between the dog in the pet shop window and his mother who is looking for coins for the parking meter in her purse.
>
> His mother turns to look at Benjamin and says, "What, honey?"
>
> Benjamin says, "Doggy" in a calm voice as he points to the dog in the window. The mother turns to look at the dog.
>
> The mother says, "He sure likes to play with that ball, doesn't he?"
>
> Benjamin nods his head in response.

The first use of *doggy* is clearly an attempt to establish joint attention, which is a case of using words as a social regulator. The second use of *doggy* is an attempt to talk about the actor of the event, now a case of using words as an attempt convey meaning.

When children begin to use words meaningfully, they also begin to demonstrate that they can use words for different purposes (Chapman, 1981). They learn that words can be used to make statements, to ask questions, to express surprise, to give orders, and to persuade others. That is, simultaneous with the expression of single words, children learn how to use words to accomplish different communicative tasks. These various functions are often signalled through the use of intonational patterns. That is, the word "Doggy!" used to express surprise is produced with a different intonational pattern than the word "Doggy?" used to ask a question.

As mentioned previously in this section, many young children have a narrower understanding of words than adults. That is, they underextend or restrict the meaning of words. In contrast, it is not uncommon for the same children to overextend the meaning of some words (Benedict, 1979). Very commonly a toddler will verbally identify a male passerby in the grocery store as "Daddy," a potentially embarrassing moment for some parents. It is sometimes assumed that the child is simply too young to reliably recognize his own daddy. Recent research challenges this assumption (Bowerman, 1982). A toddler who overextends most words will admit under questioning that the man identified as daddy is not really daddy, thus showing that the difference is understood. At least two explanations for overextension in production are reasonable. First, the child may not know the word he needs, so he uses one that is similar in meaning even though it is not the "right" word. In other words, the child may not know the word *man*, so he uses the word he does know, *daddy*. Or, the child may have difficulty recalling the appropriate word even though he knows it, so *daddy* is used instead of *man*. Overextensions are most likely to occur on newly acquired or less familiar words.

It is also at this age that many parents begin to introduce their children to print. Toddlers and parents begin to read books together, to draw and share paper and pencil or crayons. Considerable research on the early development of literacy (the ability to read and write) suggests that exposing young children to print at early ages is a critical component to literacy acquisition (Teale and Sulzby, 1986). During these initial stages, book-reading may simply consist of holding books, turning pages, and talking informally about pictures. Still, the importance of even these activities can not be underestimated, for such experience allows the child to grasp the significant differences between the language used in talk and the language used in print. Early writing experiences may simply be scribbles or drawing while mother is writing her grocery list. Again, early exposure to use of paper and pencil is critical to the child's grasping the idea that marks on a page can be communicative (Harste, Woodward, and Burke, 1984).

In summary, during the period between twelve to eighteen months, children show dramatic increases in comprehension and the beginnings of single word production. During this period, children begin to develop semantic networks for the words they learn, networks that often are narrowly defined or overgeneralized. At this stage, if children overgeneralize a word, such performance usually occurs because the necessary vocabulary item is not yet known or not easily recalled. The earliest words tend to be social activity markers, expressions of politeness or words that convey information about who is doing what to whom, the state of objects, characteristics of objects, or who owns what. When communicating, toddlers tend to use words that communicate **important** information about a situation rather than use labels for old or obvious information.

Vocalization and Speech Developments

There seems to be a continuity in the phonetic characteristics of typical vocalizations occurring in the transition period between late babbling and early words (Kent and Bauer, 1985). That is, the sounds occurring most frequently in babbling are also those occurring most frequently in the child's early words. The most common vowels are mid-central and low-front vowels (/ʌ, ɛ, æ/). High vowels (/i,u/) are infrequent. Of the consonants, stops are most frequent, followed by nasals and fricatives. Interestingly, consonant frequency varies according to phonemic context. In CV syllables, stops dominate, although in VCV productions they are proportionately much less frequent. In VC syllables, fricatives and nasals dominate. There is great variability in the amount of vocalizing done by individual children, as well as in the sounds they produce, and in the degree to which those preferences are stable across time. But, not surprisingly, the transition period between babbling and early words shows a trend toward uniformity as children gain knowledge of a particular language (Vihman, Ferguson, and Elbert, 1986). That is, early on there is a great deal of variability among children in the particular sounds they produce, and in the stability of the most frequently observed sounds from one time to the next. As the children's vocabulary size approaches thirty to fifty words, there is a definite trend across children toward stability in the frequency with which particular phonemes are produced. The trend is toward phoneme preferences within the adult language being acquired. However, there is still considerable difference between adult preferences and preferences of children with fifty-word vocabularies (Vihman, 1988a). Adults' most frequent place of articulation is alveolar; for children of twelve to eighteen months, the most frequent place is labial. For adults, most consonants appear in final and medial positions; for children, there is a clear preference for initial position consonants. In any case, though, it is important to note that the phonetic forms appearing in early words seem to be a direct outgrowth of the child's babbling practice (Locke, 1986).

Connecting Words In Phrases: (Eighteen–Twenty-four Months)

What the Child Is Like

Infants at eighteen to twenty-four months of age may occasionally show overwhelming affection for their parents, or for a doll or even a new baby. But, in the next minute, they will not want to be hugged or held or have anything to do with the object of affection. Their tempers can be uneven and unpredictable with tantrums not uncommon. They may insist on having their own way in feeding and washing themselves, or they may be "grabby" about every attractive object in sight. At this age, they will often play alone contentedly if adults are near, and may become entirely engrossed in their own activities for a time. They seem to alternate between total absorption and persistence, and flitting from one activity to the next. Eighteen to twenty-four-month-olds are very active, and often enjoy running (although a bit stiffly), jumping, dancing. They can now hold two small objects in one hand, throw a small ball overhand, scribble on paper, make a three-to-six-block tower, and turn knobs. They can identify some pictures in books, find familiar objects, and match objects of the same color, shape, and size. They also like to imitate household tasks.

Communication and Language Developments

During this period, children continue to expand their understanding of conversation and their ability to comprehend and use spoken language. Around this time, the young child begins to develop semantic or meaning networks that interrelate words. Semantic networks refer to the internal process that relates forms, categories, or classes of words (*fruit*) to the individual members of that class (*apple, banana,* and *orange*). Some researchers suggest that semantic networks are not operating until age four or older. However, work by Bowerman (1988) shows that two-year-olds demonstrate confusions that illustrate knowledge of semantically related words; that is, they may make mistakes which are clearly based on a rudimentary semantic network. For instance, she noted that her child said, "Daddy *take* his pants on." rather than "Daddy *put* his pants on." Both terms refer to actions that result in a change of location for an object, a simple semantic network. What differentiates the semantic networks of two-year-olds from those of older children is their imprecision or their use of common features that may or may not be important to adults. For example, *apples* and *oranges* may be related to one another in a two-year-old's semantic network because they can be eaten, a relationship that does not figure prominently in adult or older children's networks.

Children generally first begin to use multi-word utterances in the eighteen- to twenty-four-month age range. Some children in the early stage of this multi-word process utilize placeholders. In anticipation of increased complexity, children may extend utterances with a placeholder such as *uh* or /*WIda*/ (Bloom, 1973). Examination of the function of utterances such as /*WIda*/ *car* or /*WIda*/ *mommy* clearly indicates that the syllables /*WIda*/ have no real semantic intent, but anticipate combining two words together. Such behavior is also observed when children move from two-word to three-word sentences, as in *me uh doggy*, or in utterances that anticipate inclusion of forms such as determiners and prepositions, as in *me want uh doggy* or *me put it uh vase*. These examples show how some children also produce language that is similar to that used in telegrams, so-called telegraphic speech. Investigation of two-word combinations in English-speaking children as well as in children developing Finnish, Swedish, Samoan, Spanish, French, Russian, Korean, Japanese, and Hebrew, show a restricted number of meanings being expressed in the telegraphic stage, chiefly: 1) agent + action (mommy come); 2) action + object (drive car); 3) agent + object (baby book); 4) action + location (go park); 5) entity + location (toy [on] floor); 6) possessor + possession (my teddy); 7) entity + attribute (box shiny); and 8) demonstrative + entity (dat money) (Bloom and Lahey, 1978). In other words, children around the world appear to talk about who is doing what to whom where, where things are located, characteristics of objects and events, and who owns what.

Toddlers learning English do pay careful attention to word order, which is an important dimension of spoken English. Children learn to put agents in the subject position, the action next, and other words later (Pinker, 1984). However, in some situations, children choose not to order words according to English, but according to the importance of the word to the meaning of these messages. They will often produce the most informative word first and then string others behind them (Greenfield et al., 1985). In a situation where a favorite toy is broken, a toddler may tell mommy: *broke car, me* and *fix-it, daddy*. Even at early ages communication importance may take precedence over word order conventions.

Even at one and one half to two years of age, many routes may be taken in development of two-word utterances (Bloom, Lightbown, and Hood, 1975). For example, some children tend to use nouns in two-word productions, while other children use pronouns to achieve the same meaning. Examples of pronomial use would be *I go* instead of *Bobby go*, *she go* rather than *Mommy go*, *it big* rather than *doggy big*. Later, the pronoun-users and noun-users become indistinguishable from each other, as every child learns how to use pronouns and nouns in an appropriate fashion.

Once a child has developed some sense of word order, he/she takes two more important steps. First, they develop the grammatical aspects of language that signal different communication purposes such as negation and questions (Ervin-Tripp and Miller, 1977). A child begins by learning when and where to use the alternative forms of negation, namely *no, not, never*. These forms are employed to express a myriad of meanings such as prohibition, nonexistence, rejection, and denial among others (Bloom, 1973; Pea, 1980). Children begin understanding questions with comprehension of yes-no types such as *Is my name Mary?* followed by early wh-questions (Ervin-Tripp and Miller, 1977). Children tend to learn to use *what*, *where*, and *who* questions first, and then *when, how,* and *why* questions (Bloom and Lahey, 1978).

Second, they learn to generate word refinements in English. Although learning word order is critical for the acquisition of English, refinements such as determiners, verb endings, adjective endings, and prepositions, are all ways English uses to clarify the basic meanings of sentences. Children tend to develop-*ing* first, then the prepositions *in/on*, plurals, possessives, articles, past tense, and the *to-be* and helping verbs, as in *He is nice.* or *He is running.* (Brown, 1973). Examination of performance clearly demonstrates that children focus their attention on the refinements that are consistent or regular in application, and/or on those refinements that add important information to the sentence. Attaching *-ing* is consistent in that every time you add *-ing*, you use the exact same syllable. It is also important because it adds new information to the sentence, namely, that we are talking about **now** time, not the past. These observations suggest that young children acquire word refinements that enhance communication the most. This would seem to suggest that meaning drives syntactic acquisition, rather than the reverse. In other words, children acquire those forms that have the greatest potential to convey meaning before they acquire those forms that have less potential.

In summary, the period between eighteen to twenty-four months represents increases in comprehension abilities with children attempting to establish semantic networks among words. Most networks are simple and involve dimensions that may or may not be important from the adult perspective. Productively, children progress from the single word to two- and multi-word stages. Use of placeholders may precede two-word utterances or may be employed in multi-word strings. Most two-word utterances by children are confined to a small sub-set of semantic relations, namely, who is doing what to whom, where things are located, characteristics of objects and events, and who owns what. Some children prefer to use nouns while others use pronouns to work out their multi-word utterances. Even though English word order is important, children often seem more concerned about the communication value of utterances than precise accuracy in the word order of their productions. Once children have developed a basic ability to use multi-word strings, they begin the process of developing more complex language. Initially, they focus on linguistic forms other than declarative sentences, namely, negation and question forms. They develop an appreciation for the sentence refinement strategies of English, such as determiners and word endings.

Vocalization And Speech Developments
(See Twenty-four—Thirty-six Months)

Increasing the Complexity:
(Twenty-four—Thirty-six Months)

What the Child Is Like

The twenty-four- to thirty-six-month age period can be a time of opposite extremes. Ames and Ilg (1976) and Ames, Ilg, and Haber (1982b) describe twenty-four-month-olds as gentle, friendly, and affectionate, and calmer than at eighteen months of age. This is a time of equilibrium, according to their observations. It may even lead new parents to believe that the Terrible Twos are just a part of the child development mythology. These authors likewise describe the two-and-a-half-year-old as lovable, engaging, enthusiastic, and appreciative. For the two-and-a-half-year-old, however, they also provide great detail about ways in which the child can be just the opposite. Rigid, oppositional, negative, stubborn, aggressive, tense, explosive, imperious, tyrannical, bossy, whiny, and demanding are adjectives collected from a number of sources [cited above] describing the less-than-pleasant side of living with a twenty-four to thirty-six month-old. It seems fairly unlikely that the calm suddenly evaporates as the child is blowing out the candles on his or her thirty-month birthday cake. But from the safety of the "Three's," there may be a time in the "Two's" that parents can look back on as more chaotic than others.

Basically, the problem seems to be that two-year-olds insist on doing things their own way. They like routines and sequences and often demand that things are ritualistically done "just so" (as they have been done previously)—whether or not the insisted-upon procedure fits a particular circumstance. For example, because it once made sense to remove a shoe to get clothes off in the bathroom, they will always want to take off one shoe before using the toilet. Or, because they once were given raisins to put in their cereal, they will always have to have raisins to put in their cereal—and they had better be given to them in a little red box each time, too!

Two-year-olds have very limited self control, and are not particularly good at waiting, hurrying, sharing, or changing activities. They may also pit parents against each other, often wanting the parent who is **not** there at the moment. And, they can begin to show some wiliness as they learn to manipulate things to get what they want. If one parent says no, they may immediately ask the other. Or, an older "Two" may ask the dolly if **she** wants some candy, and when the doll inevitably says "yes," the child presents what is now the doll's request to the parent. If, somehow, parents can generally find the resources to deal with the dark moments of this age with humor, kindness, and (above all!) patience, then there is a chance the child will occasionally give in. If the parent responds to the child's behaviors with harsh, unrelenting demands, they may simply see more of the same. Fortunately or not, "Two's" learn much by imitating the behaviors they see, hear, and experience.

One of the great characteristics of twenty-four to thirty-six-month-olds is that they generally bounce back fairly quickly from even the most ferocious conflict situations. And then they are their loving, engaging, enthusiastic—and increasingly knowledgable and competent—selves. They run with confidence and ease, jump with both feet, balance on one foot, dance to music, turn door handles, and some can even ride tricycles. They show much more independence in feeding, dressing, and toileting themselves. They especially enjoy playing with water, sand, and play dough. They also enjoy stories, songs, and rhymes, and often want to hear favorite ones long after the parents do. Children of this age generally play near, but not **with** other children except for short periods of time. They often initiate their own play activities, and engage in quite a lot of pretending and make-believe play.

Two-year-olds can solve some simple problems, and occasionally anticipate consequences. They know how a great number of toys and household objects turn, move, and work. Their increasing competencies and agility, combined with an interest in exploring everything, a drive to imitate, very little sense of danger, and an insistence on doing things their own way, can create some hair-raising experiences for even the most vigilant of parents. It is, to say the least, an exciting and challenging time.

Communication and Language Developments

Children of this age develop more and more language to converse on a variety of topics for longer periods of time. Children with less language tend to jump from topic to topic, while those with more language can stay on the same topic for dozens of exchanges. During this period, children learn how to open conversations, how to terminate conversations, and how to introduce topics verbally. They no longer need to resort to gestures or the nonverbal context to clarify what they are talking about. Words will accomplish the task. Now the child can begin to talk about the past and about the future (Sachs, 1983; Miller and Sperry, 1988) with utterances such as: *Remember when we play toys last night.* or *I want go to circus next week.*

Two- to three-year-old children show that they know how to use talk for different reasons. They can pick a topic and tell a story or share an experience about it. They can also describe and explain. Among the variety of purposes for communication, the three aforementioned have been the most researched in twenty-four to thirty-six-month-olds.

Telling stories or sharing experiences requires that the child order events chronologically and engage in discourse about how they feel about those events (Peece, 1987). Very young children often tell stories by giving the end of the story followed by the beginning and then the middle (Brown, 1976). As the child matures, he inserts intervening steps along with comments and feelings. For instance, children may start with stories such as: "I saw a clown." This might lead to stories such as: "I saw a clown and I went to the circus." Next, "Daddy and Mommy and Sarah went to the circus. Daddy bought pink cotton candy. I got all sticky. The clown gave me a doggy balloon. I laugh and laugh and laugh and laugh. I was scared of the bears." This process of refining and elaborating stories proceeds throughout the preschool and into the school-age years.

In addition to telling stories or sharing experiences, children also learn how to give instructions. Giving clear instructions requires providing a step-by-step procedure to lead to completion of a particular task. Each step must include only those variables critical to the completion of the task. In addition, it is the speaker's responsibility to make sure that the listener knows that he is being given instructions. When children first begin to give instructions, they often proceed without telling others what their purpose is (Freedle and Hale, 1979). In addition, young children often fail to include all the important steps and more importantly they frequently fail to distinguish between germane and insignificant information. For instance, one child may tell another that to make candy "You need a blue bowl." The second child may not have a blue bowl and, being unable to make candy, walk away. As with story telling, children learn all the aspects of giving directions over the course of the preschool and early elementary years.

In addition to telling stories and giving directions, young children learn how to provide descriptions. Clear descriptions should start with the most salient point of the item and then progress systematically to other salient points that distinguish that item, person, or event from all others. In early descriptions, children often begin with a single descriptive statement that focuses on the most salient aspect for them (Lindfors, 1980). As the description unfolds, more details are added in an unorganized fashion. Later the child realizes that the details need to be systematic and that they should reflect the aspects that are salient to others.

As the child matures through the second year, he continues to develop more words, to refine the meanings of the words he knows, and to develop even more sophisticated semantic networks. Children also learn an important idea about meaning, namely, that words can be used to tease or they can be used to create a new reality (Fein and Moarin, 1985). For instance, in play, it is not uncommon for two-year-old children to take a cup, place it on their head, and call it a *hat*. At least two possible results can follow. Either the child can start to laugh indicating that the use of this word was to provoke or to tease, or the child can begin to parade around as if she were modeling the hat indicating that reality is changed. In the latter case, the cup is indeed a hat. The ability to change reality is important since it forms the basis for features of figurative language (Winner, 1979) such as metaphor and simile, which will be fully mastered much later in the child's development.

Previously, we noted that eighteen- to twenty-four-month-old children progress from single words to multi-word utterances and to use sentence refinements such as grammatical prefixes and suffixes. During the period from two and three years of age, children learn how to add and combine other information to make more complex sentences. In English, meaning complexity is achieved by three syntactic mechanisms (Clark and Clark, 1979). First, we can employ coordination. This involves adding new information to the sentence through the use of words such as *and*, *because*, and *but*. Second, we can employ relativization. This involves adding new information to the nouns of sentences using such words as *who, which,* and *that,* resulting in sentences such as: *I know the boy who is eating the ice cream cone.* Third, we can employ complementation. This involves inserting new information into sentences, resulting in sentences such as: *He likes to go to the circus.* The base sentence means *He likes something,* with which the new information *He goes to the circus,* has been combined. Once children begin to notice complexity, they develop each of these three systems in their own communication.

At approximately two and a half years, children are observed to conjoin thoughts in single sentences. The simplest, and most frequent, way this is achieved is through the use of the conjunction *and* (Bloom, Lahey, Hood, Lifter, and Fiess, 1980). In combining thoughts, one can express them as phrases as in *I want Mommy and Daddy . . . .* , or as complete sentences as in *I went to the store and bought some apples. .* Children use phrase combining or coordination long before they use sentence coordination (Bloom et al., 1980; Tager-Flusberg, de Villiers, and Hakuta, 1982). The choice of these constructions is tied to the context in which they are used (Jeremy, 1978). Phrasal coordination tends to be used when events occurred simultaneously or in the same location. If the events took place in different locations and different times, then sentence coordination is more likely. This latter observation shows clearly that young children are sensitive to communication situations.

Children also pay attention to other types of coordination such as coordination to mark simultaneous time, *That hurts when you touch it,* to mark cause and effect, *He fell down because he slipped,* and to mark opposition of events, *He wears diapers but I don't,* (Bloom et al., 1980). As children begin to express these more complex notions, they initially employ *and* rather than the appropriate form. This results in early productions such as, *That hurts and you touch it,* for simultaneous time, as, *He fell down and he slipped,* for cause and effect relations, and *He wears diapers and I don't,* for opposition. When children use language which is complex or new to them, they often use previously mastered syntactic forms to express new meanings (Slobin, 1973). Since the earliest conjunction acquired by children is *and,* it should not be surprising that they use this form to express a variety of new meanings. Such use, though syntactically incorrect from an adult perspective, should be honored as the child's best effort to communicate complex ideas. As the children become more comfortable with the semantic requirements of complex language, they will acquire linguistic forms that are like the adult version.

In addition to coordination, two- to three-year-olds also begin to develop mastery of the process of relativization, or the addition of new information to the noun of a sentence in order to specify that noun. The earliest forms developed by children to express this complexity involve possessive pronouns and embedded adjectives (Bloom and Lahey, 1978). In order to specify which object or event they are concerned about, they use expressions such as *his ball* or *red ball*. Later, prepositional phrases are used to specify objects, particularly the preposition *with* which yields constructions such as *The girl with hat* (Clark and Carpenter, 1989). Between three and four years of age, acquisition of traditional relative clauses using words like [who], [that], or [which] can be observed. Even then the introducing word is often omitted, or [and] is used, as in, *I see boy run down the street*, or *I see boy and he running down street*. (Bloom et al., 1980). Young children also tend to add the relative clause to the end of the sentence rather than the middle, yielding utterances such as, *I see boy and he running down the street*, before sentences like, *The girl me like is pretty*. (Limber, 1973). In the first sentence, the relative clause, *and he running down the street* is attached to the end of the sentence and comments on the noun *boy*. In the second sentence, the relative clause, *me like* comments on the noun, *the girl* and is embedded in the middle of the sentence. The first type of sentence is also understood by two- to three-year-olds before they understand the second type (Hamburger and Crain, 1982).

In addition to coordination and relativization, children in the two- to three-year age range begin to develop complementation which refers to the insertion of new relationships into sentences as part of those sentences. The earliest and most common forms of complementation are infinitives such as *wanna* or *gonna* as in *Me wanna go town* (Bloom and Lahey, 1978). From these early infinitives, children develop what are called perceptual verb complements (Bloom, Ripsoli, Gartner, and Hafitz, 1989). Perceptual verb complements involve verbs such as *think*, *see*, *look*, and *know*. Children seem to use certain complement forms with specific perceptual verbs. For instance, children have been noted to use only *that* with the perceptual verb *think* resulting in utterances such as *I think that me go circus*, while the perceptual verb *know* only takes *what* clauses, as in *I know what is in this bag*. With *see* and *look*, both types of clauses are common, although in both instances the [what] clauses are observed to exceed the [that] clauses. Other types of complementation do not tend to appear until after age three.

As can be seen from the examples provided in this section, when children do begin to use complex language, they often produce sentences that do not conform entirely to adult versions of the same sentences. Child language should be appreciated as an important stepping stone to the subsequent acquisition of mature adult expressions, rather than as a collection of grammar "mistakes."

It is also important to recognize that different children may arrive at the same point in complex language acquisition, by rather different routes (Peters, 1983). Some children build complexities word-by-word and could be described as piece-meal learners. Other children develop the whole form and then later break these wholes down into their individual parts. These latter children can be described as holistic or gestalt learners. In examining the productions of these two groups of children, piece-meal learners are often observed to produce sentences with many grammatical "mistakes" while gestalt learners do not. As a consequence, piece-meal learners are often seen as being less advanced linguistically than gestalt learners. In contrast, because gestalt learners break down the wholes later, their production of grammatical "errors" may be seen as a regression in the acquisition of syntactic forms. Neither conclusion is warranted. The only conclusion that can be derived is that different children acquire complex language in different ways and both piece-meal and gestalt learning are acceptable means of achieving this goal.

In summary, the period between twenty-four to thirty-six months involves the considerable development of conversational abilities. Children learn to greet, to terminate, to topicalize, and to carry on extended conversations. In addition, they learn to use language for different purposes, most importantly to tell stories or share experiences, to give directions, to describe, and to use language to change reality or pretend. Children in this stage are also learning to express the primary ways in which English makes complex sentences, namely, coordination, relativization, and complementation. Initially, these productions may evidence forms that are not in concert with adult forms, but they should be honored as legitimate attempts by the child to develop complex language. Some of these inconsistencies are due to omissions of key grammatical elements, or the use of previously learned syntactic forms to express new meanings in language. As was true with previous stages of language development, children use alternative strategies to acquire complex language. Some children build their language step-by-step, while others acquire the whole form and then work out the details later.

Vocalization and Speech Developments

Since the 1930's, there have been numerous attempts to establish developmental norms for phoneme acquisition by children from the time they begin using words at about one year of age. These studies have been both cross-sectional and longitudinal, and have been fraught with methodological and theoretical problems. Vihman (1988b) provides an excellent comparative discussion. In the cross-sectional studies, there are marked differences in sample size, sample characteristics, manner of collecting the sample (i.e. whether it is spontaneous or imitated speech), word positions examined, and criteria for "age of acquisition." However, results of the studies do agree enough to provide a general picture of the order of acquisition. First of all, vowels and diphthongs are usually acquired by the age of three. Of the consonants, nasals (/n, m, ng/), stops (/p, t, k, b, d, g/), and glides (/w, j/) are all customarily used at the age of two years, and are generally considered to be mastered by age three. The liquids (/l,r/) are customarily used by age three, but may not be mastered until over four years of age. Customary use of fricatives (/sh, v, z, z, ð, θ) begins at thirty-six months or older, and may not be mastered until after four years of age. Interestingly, the /s/ fricative is customarily used early (by about twenty-four months) and is mastered before other fricatives (by forty-four months). It should be noted that the term "customary use" refers to correct production in two out of three word positions by 51 percent of the children tested; and "mastery" refers to correct production in all three word positions by 90 percent of the children (Prather, Hedrick, and Kern, 1975). These are strict criteria, and thus reflect the upper age limits for production, rather than average performance. That is, many children will be using the sounds, at least occasionally, long before the ages mentioned. However, the sequence is valid, and the ages are a general guideline for when it is reasonable to expect that the child's production will be similar to the adult model.

A different, and relatively recent, approach to the study of child phonology is the study of phonological processes. (See reviews in Ingram, 1986; Vihman, 1988b.) Children make systematic errors in their attempts to produce adult words. These are grouped according to whether the word or syllable structure has been simplified (whole word processes), or whether phonological segments have been substituted for each other (segment substitution processes). Some examples of each follow:

I. Whole Word Processes
    A. Reduction Processes
        1. Syllable deletion: saying "banana" as "nana" /naenae/
        2. Consonant deletion: saying "Zak" as "Za" /zae/
        3. Consonant cluster reduction: saying "Frank" as "Fank" /faenk/
    B. Assimilatory Processes
        1. Reduplication: saying "kitty" as "kiki" /kiki/
        2. Consonant harmony: saying "doggie" as "goggie" /g> gI/

II. Segment Substitution Processes
        1. Velar fronting: saying "key" as "tee" /ti/
        2. Gliding: saying "rabbit" as "wabbit" /waebIt/
        3. Stopping: saying "thumb" as "tumb" /t∧m/

These error processes occur with great regularity in the speech of young normally developing children. In general, the simplifying processes are not much used after the age of three (Vihman and Greenlea, 1987). Common exceptions are that consonant clusters are still routinely reduced, and fricatives and liquids often substituted by other elements. But by school-age, basic articulatory mastery is complete for normally developing children (Vihman, 1988b).

5

Infant and Toddler Auditory "Work"

It is the province of knowledge to speak
and it is the privilege of wisdom to listen.
(Oliver Wendell Holmes, *The Poet at the Breakfast Table*, 1872)

This chapter is about the spoken sounds the child hears, and eventually learns to understand and produce. If only the processes of listening, comprehending, and talking could be so simple. . . . But, of course, they are not. In the first place, what the child hears is not the same thing as what the child listens to. Secondly, what the child listens to, he or she may or may not understand. And thirdly, what the child understands, he may or may not be able to (or choose to) say. Since the target behaviors in this book are the complex ones of listening, understanding, and using spoken language, then why this chapter on work on the auditory dimension alone? The answer is twofold:

1. Why auditory? Audition is treated separately in this chapter in order to provide background information about the primacy of the auditory channel for learning spoken language, about nor-

mal expectations for auditory abilities in young children, and about the auditory process itself.

2. Why auditory "work"? There are a number of vitally important strategies for encouraging growth in both auditory and speech abilities in very young hearing-impaired children that can be integrated into the child's normal everyday interacting and play with the important adults in his or her life. This "work," which obviously must really be "play" in order to keep the child's interest, can be expected to have extremely beneficial results over time.

The Primacy of Audition

In terms of sensory experience, spoken language is primarily an acoustic event (Erber, 1982; Fry, 1978; Ling, 1976; Ling and Ling, 1978; Pollack, 1985; Sanders, 1982). Clearly, some parts of a spoken message have redundant representation in the visual and tactile modalities which may need to be used by some hearing-impaired children as a supplement to audition. But since spoken language is acoustically based, the ears are the most useful and efficient sense modality for its reception. (It is assumed that cochlear implants employ audition in the sense that the term is used in this chapter.)

The effect of hearing impairment is to reduce the amount of acoustic information available. Depending upon its severity, hearing loss is likely to distort or eliminate a number of acoustic cues. However, hearing impairment is rarely total. It has long been technologically possible to provide amplification with the potential of permitting the majority of hearing-impaired children to learn to use their residual hearing (Boothroyd, 1970; Ling, 1964). And with recent advances in the power and clarity of hearing aids and in the precision of fitting, the use of audition in the reception of spoken language is within reach of the majority of children with severe-to-profound hearing losses. Naturally, the more hearing the child has, the more acoustic cues are available. However, even with minimal hearing (e.g. aided hearing within the speech range at only 250 and 500 Hz), the child can learn to perceive and monitor durational, rhythmic, and intonation cues. The result can be improved understanding, as well as improved intelligibility and predictability in the child's own speech. Markides (1986) has eloquently described the history of the use of residual hearing for educating the hearing-impaired. The first recorded (and as Markides says, rather drastic) attempts were those of Archigene (98-117 A.D.) who tried to stimulate residual hearing by blowing a trumpet in the deaf person's ear. However, publications concerned with utilization of residual hearing in very young hearing-impaired children, or with a "critical period" for learning to listen, are a rather more recent phenomenon (Fry, 1966; Griffiths, 1964; Horton, 1974; Pollack, 1970; Tervoort, 1964; Whetnall, 1958). There is additional supportive evidence for the importance of early auditory stimulation in studies of sensory deprivation using animals (Tees, 1967; Riesen, 1974). One of the first attempts to explore systematically the effects of early auditory stimulation for hearing-impaired children was that of Griffiths (1955). This study compared the speech of a group of children aided at a mean age of three years, eight months with a group aided at a mean age of five years, three months. The speech of the earlier-aided children was rated as more normal and more intelligible by four separate panels of judges. But even the earlier-aided children in this study would be considered very late-aided by today's standards. Since Griffiths' study, other research has been done which strongly supports the contention that early auditory stimulation has beneficial effects on speech reception, speech intelligibility, language development, and academic achievement (Griffiths and Ebbin, 1978; Ling, Leckie, Pollack, Simser, and Smith, 1981; Ling and Milne, 1981; Luterman, 1976; Pollack and Ernst; 1974; Stone, 1983). But studies of this issue with very young hearing-impaired human subjects are methodologically difficult to design and implement. One relatively minor problem is that of trying to assemble large enough groups of very young hearing-impaired subjects who are similar on relevant variables (e.g. age, degree of hearing loss, age at detection, age when full-time wearing of amplification was begun, degree and nature of parental involvement). Then there is the problem of defining in an experimental sense exactly what an auditory emphasis or auditory stimulation is. Related to that is the problem of attempting to standardize how the work is implemented and measured in a rigorous, as well as educationally meaningful, manner. All of these problems contribute to the ultimate difficulty of separating the effects of early *auditorally based* intervention from the effects of early intervention of any kind.

Audition: What Develops?

Prenatal Hearing

The issues of how much a fetus can hear, and when he or she hears it, are only partially understood at present. According to Busnel and Granier-Deferre (1983), most researchers accept the contention that a seven-month-old fetus demonstrates reliable behavioral reactions to sound. In fact, this is probably a conservative estimate. All of the inner ear anatomical structures are present in the fetus at six months, and the cochlear receptors are ready to function even at four months gestational age. On the other hand, anatomical presence does not necessarily imply working capacity, and there is a lack of experimental data to confirm the beginning of audition in prenatal humans. In order for audition to occur, complex nervous connections must be made between various subcortical structures, as well as myelinization of nerve fibers, formation of a sufficient number of synapses, and various enzymatic activities initiated. Knowledge of exactly when all of these aspects are fully functioning in the fetus is incomplete. Our knowledge of central (neural) development is, in fact, also incomplete for the postnatal infant (Gorga, Kaminski, Beauchaine, Jesteadt, Neeley, 1989).

One of the complicating factors in prenatal hearing research is that the transmission characteristics of the fluid environment of the fetal auditory system are little understood (Kuhl, 1987). What is known is that externally produced sounds below 1000 Hz are attenuated very little in the uterus (Busnel and Granier-Deferre, 1983). Since the prosodic characteristics of the mother's voice would be preserved under those conditions, this is seen as a possible explanation for the baby's recognition and preference for the mother's voice over the voices of other women very soon after birth (DeCasper and Fifer, 1980).

Postnatal Hearing

The research on (postnatal) infant hearing can be categorized according to its focus either on auditory sensitivity (threshold measures) or on auditory responses to speech as a social signal. These will be considered in turn.

With regard to **auditory sensitivity**, Wilson and Gerber (1983) contend that there is no, or very little, documented evidence for development across age in behavioral responses to sound. They state that changes in thresholds that have been observed by others (Northern and Downs, 1978; Sweitzer, 1977; Thompson and Weber, 1974) are probably measurement artifacts, primarily related to the lack of use of complex reinforcers.

But precise knowledge of auditory thresholds in normally hearing infants prior to one year of age is sketchy and contradictory. Wilson and Gerber's data show relative stability in children's responses (at 20 to 30 dB HL) to warble tones at 500, 1000, and 4000 Hz from five months of age on. However, there is some additional evidence suggesting an improvement in low frequency hearing (presumably 250 Hz) between six months and twelve months of age. At six months, low frequency hearing may differ from adult hearing by as much as 20 to 25 dB (Schneider, Trehub, and Bull, 1979; Trehub and Schneider, 1983; Trehub, Schneider, and Endman, 1980; Wilson and Gerber, 1983); at twelve months, it approximates that of adults. It has been hypothesized that, rather than being due to changes in inner ear sensitivity, the apparent improvement may be attributed to a high incidence of undetected middle ear pathology in the infants, or to anatomical changes in the characteristics of the child's conductive system (growth in the external auditory canal, pinna, tympanic membrane) which change its resonance characteristics. This observation of relatively poor low-frequency thresholds conflicts with previous electrophysiological data that suggest better low-frequency hearing than high in infancy (Hecox, 1975).

Another possible developmental change in auditory responses is the finding that infants at six months of age are poorer at listening tasks in noisy situations than they are at twenty-four months. Their responses to speech are 10 to 12 dB worse; to a 4000 Hz octave band noise, 20 dB worse (Schneider, Trehub, and Bull, 1980). This may partially explain why in moderately noisy conditions, infants fail to notice some signals that are clearly audible to adults. Naturally, adults' knowledge of context cues (and language), as well as their understanding and motivation to respond, must contribute to the observed differences.

In any case, there is little behavioral data regarding auditory thresholds (sensitivity) of infants *under* five months of age. Interestingly, a number of the studies related to infants' **auditory responses to**

speech as a social signal provide data on infants well under that age. However, these data do not attempt to trace developmental trends. The focus is more on searching for the origins of various kinds of auditory perceptual abilities. For example, this research has shown that three-day-old infants demonstrate a preference for their own mothers' highly intonated voices (DeCasper and Fifer, 1980); this had been previously demonstrated with four- to six-week-old infants (Mehler, Bertoncini, Barriere, and Jassik-Geschenfeld, 1978). In fact, studies using only the fundamental frequency of the mother's normal speaking voice caused the infant to demonstrate the same preference (Kuhl, 1981). Sensitivity to intraphonemic categorical difference has been observed in infants at one month of age (Eimas, Siqueland, Jusczyk, and Vigorito, 1971) and hemispheric assymetries for speech signals at two months of age (Best, Hoffman, and Glanville, 1982). By six months of age, infants equate phonetically identical sounds even when the sounds are produced by different speakers in different tones of voice, and in different phonemic contexts (Kuhl, 1983).

Many of these studies of infant auditory perceptual abilities were undertaken in order to shed light on the continuing debate regarding the origins of the abilities: that is, the degree to which the abilities are innate or learned (the same nature/nurture controversy discussed in Chapter 2). The debate rages on. But there is overwhelming agreement about one item: Very young infants are remarkably responsive to speech, and they demonstrate a number of abilities that, logically, must facilitate the learning of spoken language. These early auditory abilities include near-adult threshold sensitivities, recognition of the mother's voice, and perception of phonemic category differences and similarities. The existence of these abilities provides excellent support for the importance of early detection of hearing loss. That is, it can be assumed that the earlier the wearing of hearing aids, the more equal the chance that the hearing-impaired infant will use these same abilities to begin sorting out the stream of spoken language around him. One thing is absolutely certain: without amplification, the abilities are not being utilized by the hearing-impaired infant.

Auditory "Skills" and Auditory Processing Models

All of the informed auditory training work done with hearing-impaired children to develop auditory skills is based on theoretical models and constructs. As Sanders (1982) says, we are far from comprehensive knowledge of the intricate process of human communication, including the precise role of audition in that process. Many of the relevant questions and issues have so far proven to be so complex as to "defy experimental study within the limits of current knowledge and equipment" (p. 16). For example, we really do not have certain knowledge of exactly how humans formulate ideas, encode them in language, perceive and analyze acoustic signals, and process linguistic messages produced by others. However, based on research, empirical data, and reasoning, hypothetical models have been developed that integrate existing pieces of knowledge and thinking. The researcher's intention is that the models' integrity and usefulness will then be experimentally tested and accordingly revised—not that the component units are necessarily ready to be treated as realities upon which to base intervention practice. However, the habilitationist cannot wait for scientific knowledge to be complete, and sometimes the practitioner's zeal for certainty embues the theoretical constructs with more reality than they deserve. Perhaps the essential thought to bear in mind is that the auditory processing "whole" is greater than the sum of current knowledge of its hypothesized parts.

Several excellent auditory processing models are presented and explained in Bergman (1985), Doehring (1983), Kuhl (1979, 1987), Ling (1978), and Sanders (1982). Some of the hypothetical components of commonly agreed-upon stages will be mentioned, and then implications illustrated for hearing-impaired children.

For an overview of the sequence, let us assume that the child's peripheral ear has received a bit of speech/acoustic information and the that child was *motivated* to *attend* to it (or to *detect* it). According to the auditory processing models cited above, there is first some sort of frequency, intensity, and time analysis done by the peripheral ear, with transformation of the input into representative neural patterns. Brief sensory memory storage must be occurring at this stage in order for the analysis and transformation to take place. Next, it is known that some preliminary auditory processing occurs in the brainstem related to *localization*, and separation of competing messages (i.e. *selective listening* or *selective attention*). And finally, when the auditory cortex receives the input, higher levels of analysis occur about which we have the least certain knowledge and, consequently, the most theorizing. This processing presumably includes phonetic, phonological, syntactic, semantic, and pragmatic/contextual processing. It may very well require hypothesized cortical activities such as the following: *discriminating* from close cognates, *identifying* (*categorizing* or *associating*) with other similar items, and *comprehending* (*integrating* or *interpreting*) as meaning is derived. And clearly, both short-term and long-term *memory* are essential to this higher level processing of auditory/linguistic messages.

The preceding discussion has highlighted a number of items that are featured in most texts and curricula as the content or goals of auditory training for hearing-impaired children (Erber, 1982; Hirsch, 1970; Los Angeles County Public Schools' Auditory Skills Curriculum, 1976; Ling, 1978; Lowell and Stoner, 1960; Northcott, 1978; Pollack, 1985; Sitnick, Rushmer, and Arpan, 1977). Particularly in view of the additional concurrence of scholarly opinion in including these items in their models, it seems reasonable to assume that each of these components is involved in some manner or at some level in processing spoken language. And it may be beneficial (with a particular child, or at given points in time, or as part of a specific game or activity) to focus on one auditory dimension alone. **But these components overlap and interrelate in both natural and structured activities to such a degree that they cannot seriously be considered to be discrete or necessarily hierarchical** (Ling, 1986; Sanders, 1982). Curricula which attempt to train these as isolated auditory "skills" may play a useful role for the teacher of older children in that the curricula systematize instructional objectives and activities related to improving the child's use of residual hearing. But isolated rote training on hypothetical auditory subskills is generally inappropriate—and unnecessary—with hearing-impaired children under three years of age.

For the young child, the ability to demonstrate capability concerning any of the highlighted auditory components is inextricably linked to the child's cognitive and spoken language growth. That is, for the toddler to be motivated to attend selectively; to localize; to discriminate; to identify, categorize, associate; to integrate, interpret, comprehend—for all of these, there must be meaning attached to the event. And, to paraphrase Winnie-the-Pooh (Milne, 1926), the main place that meaning in acoustic input comes from is from Gradual Acquisition of Spoken Language. And the main place spoken language comes from is from Normal, Everyday Interacting and Play with Caregivers Using Spoken Language. This is not to imply a lack of planning or structure in the intervention or the interacting processes. For example, simply being aware of the importance of consistently noticing relevant sounds or remarking on the child's noticing them could be viewed as introducing a "structured" or contrived element into a conversational interaction between caregiver and child. Certainly, parents of normally hearing children also notice sounds and notice their children's reactions to them. But parents of hearing-impaired children become especially conscious of the importance of these particular events for encouraging the child's use of his or her residual hearing, and consequently they attempt to do both kinds of noticing consistently, and perhaps with a bit more deliberate interest and enthusiasm.

The following fifteen-second scene may illustrate these points more clearly.

- The context. . . .

   A father and his fourteen-month-old son are building with blocks on the floor in the living room after supper. The child has a severe-to-profound sensori-neural hearing loss, and has been wearing hearing aids consistently for two months. The mother has been in another room, but at the beginning of this scene appears in the doorway which is about six feet away from the child. The child is playing beside his father, with his back to the doorway in which the mother is now standing.

- The action. . . .

   Mother waits for a break in the conversation between father and son, and then calls, "Tony!"

   The father ceases block-building, leans toward Tony, puts his head to one side as his face takes on an interested, curious sort of "listening" expression. He says, "Listen! Did you hear that? I heard something." Tony has been looking at the father's face from the time the father stopped playing with the blocks and leaned forward. When his father continues to maintain the "listening" expression without saying or doing more, Tony looks back at the blocks and picks up one to start playing again.

   The mother pauses a second or two, and then calls again, "Tony!"

   Tony looks up, alertly, at the father.

The father says nothing, but still looks as if he is listening to something.

His mother takes a step forward, and calls once more, "Tony! Time for your bath!"

This time, Tony turns around and sees his mother. She smiles and says, "Terrific! You heard me. It's time for your bath."

Tony smiles impishly, and toddles off, full speed, in the opposite direction.

- The explanation. . . .

Mother waits for a break in the conversation between father and son, and then calls, "Tony!"

The mother's voice is loud enough to be well within this particular child's range of hearing, so that it is reasonable for the child to *detect* it. Since the mother is six feet away, which is much further than a normal conversational distance, this could be viewed as an instance of a *distance listening* event. She has waited for a break in their conversation, partly because it is conversationally appropriate to do so, and partly because Tony stands a better chance of hearing her if her calling voice occurs in quiet. This is an effort to enhance the *figure* (signal) relative to the *ground* (noise). Some children, perhaps at a more advanced stage, may be expected to hear a calling voice in this sort of situation even when there is other talking going on. In fact, in any normal everyday situation in the home, there is quite likely to be other noise in the room (e.g. from the toys at hand, from the street outside, from the dishwasher, from an older sibling turning pages in a book) which will be reaching the microphone of the child's hearing aid and being amplified. The signal, for example, the calling voice, must be louder than the surrounding noise in order for the child to detect it. The degree to which it is louder will be the degree to which it is easier for the child to hear. This simple fact is often easily forgotten in the course of normal activities where, for example, the radio or TV may be left on for long periods of time. In a sense, nearly all normal everyday listening involves *selective attention* or *selective listening* abilities.

The father ceases block-building, leans toward Tony, puts his head to one side as his face takes on an inter-

ested, curious sort of "listening" expression. He says, "Listen! Did you hear that? I heard something." Tony has been looking the father's face from the time the father stopped playing with the blocks and leaned forward. When his father continues to maintain the "listening" expression without saying or doing more, Tony looks back at the blocks and picks up one to start playing again.

The father's behaviors are an attempt to *alert* Tony and *motivate* him to *attend*. Depending upon the degree of the child's hearing loss, his absorption in a task, and his or her backlog of positive experiences listening, he or she may respond immediately to a calling voice from six feet away. Others will need to be alerted to listen. As for the "listening" expression, it is impossible to actually present an appearance of listening that is unmistakable as listening. That is, one person cannot see another person hearing or listening. But it is possible to see the listener's reaction to sound, and interest or curiosity about it, which is what the father is demonstrating here.

The mother pauses a second, and then calls again, "Tony!"

In this particular instance, a certain number of repetitions of the mother's calling seems reasonable. However, the real goal is clearly for the child to respond after only one instance of the mother calling. If parents and professionals always quickly give the child multiple repetitions of messages or task demands, the child may come to expect that a second or third repetition is coming, and may not bother to respond initially. One simple-minded, but vitally important strategy which may lead toward the child's responding after being called once (or after being asked to perform any kind of task, for that matter) is the one of being certain to provide ample time for the child to respond before calling again. (Of course, this is also important from a conversational, turn-taking perspective.) It is equally important to recognize that there are times when the child is not going to respond, and to stop repeating oneself long before it becomes a pointlessly frustrating exercise. Before that, however, there are several steps described below which one can take when it is necessary to enhance the audibility of the acoustic signal.

> **Tony looks up, alertly, at the father.**
> **The father says nothing, but still looks as if he is listening to something.**

This suggests that Tony *detected* a voice from the surrounding background noise (*selective attention*), but has incorrectly (but not surprisingly) assumed it was his father speaking to him. He has thus *localized* the sound incorrectly in that he thought it came from in front rather than in back of himself. He is also not attending sufficiently to the higher fundamental frequency and harmonic cues which, one day, will tell him that it was his mother speaking and not his father. This could be viewed as a *discrimination* task, with the child being required to discriminate between his mother's and his father's voices. In situations where a large number of people could ostensibly be calling the child, the task may be more one of *identification*.

> **His mother takes a step forward, and calls once more, "Tony! Time for your bath."**
> **This time, Tony turns around and sees his mother. She smiles and says, "Terrific! You heard me. It's time for your bath."**
> **Tony smiles impishly, and toddles off, full speed, in the opposite direction.**

The mother's behaviors are intended to make her acoustic input more salient (more easily *detected*) to the child. By stepping forward, she has somewhat decreased the distance from the sound source (her mouth), to the microphone on the child's hearing aid. This will make the sound a bit louder. By also adding the sentence "Time for your bath!," she has provided a longer piece of acoustic input. The child may not be able to *understand* this bit of information auditorally, but the mother's primary purpose here is simply to provide a lengthier clue to the child to help in his *localizing* (the source of the calling voice) and *associating* (that voice = mother) tasks. Naturally, it is important that she has used a contextually and prosodically appropriate, semantically meaningful, and syntactically correct sentence. These aspects of her input will eventually lead to Tony's *understanding*. And by doing all of these things in all of the hundreds of small events which occur in a day, the mother is building up Tony's belief that he is *expected* to understand spoken messages, with or (often) without looking at the speaker's face. In addition, Tony's mother has rewarded his turning by smiling and by using words which describe exactly what it was that he did that was pleasing. These parent responses are intended to be part of motivating Tony to want to listen the next time(s).

One interpretation of Tony's behavior in this scene could be that Tony soon detected the sound, localized it to a source behind himself, identified the mother as the speaker, and comprehended the verbal message. Another interpretation could be that Tony detected the voice, saw that it was not his father speaking, began searching visually for the sound source, and happened to find his mother in the process. Then he saw the pyjamas in her hand, and knowing what that meant, toddled off. In a research study, it might be important to determine which of these interpretations is correct. But in a real life situation, it doesn't much matter. The parents are not testing his ability to perform listening tasks. In this normal, everyday event, they are rather, providing all the conditions which are likely to encourage and promote Tony's use of residual hearing. These include the provision of appropriate "input" in terms of the prosody, intensity, syntax, semantics, and conversational context. The conditions also include provision of motivation and social or circumstantial "rewards." If, this time, Tony saw his mother in the course of visual searching for "a voice-not-father's," then this experience will simply be part of the learning process. If he did actually localize the source and identify the speaker auditorally, then this experience is an example of his having learned. Either way, at every future opportunity, the parents will continue to make the same effort to "set up" events in such a way as to allow, encourage, and expect Tony to listen.

This next scene is an example of a normal, everyday interactive event between a mother and her slightly older child. The mother smoothly and automatically employs a number of strategies to encourage the child to listen.

- The context. . . .

    This child is twenty-three months of age, has a severe-to-profound sensori-neural hearing loss, and has worn aids consistently since eleven months of age. Consequently, she has a "hearing age" of twelve months. The mother and child are playing on the kitchen floor with blocks, cars, and little people dolls. They have just built a very tall tower with the blocks. (The event took about thirty seconds in all.)

● The action. . . .

Tamara says, "Where block?" as she looks around for another block on the floor. She is standing since the tower they are building is so tall.

Guessing what Tamara meant, the mother says, "Where's another block?" Tamara is not watching the mother's face since she is still searching for blocks.

Tamara says, " 'Nother block?"

Mother says, "Hmmm—well let's see." Mother looks for more blocks; Tamara turns away. "Oh—here's one." Tamara turns back, and the mother hands her a block.

The mother then says, "Thank you."

Tamara says, "What?" and looks at her mother.

The mother rubs her nose, partially obscuring her mouth, and says, "You can say 'Thank you.'"

Tamara again says, "What?"

This time the mother lets Tamara look at her face as she says, "You're supposed to say 'Thank you.'"

Tamara repeats, "Thank you."

Tamara puts the block on the top of the teetering tower, which then topples. She steps back [right on the mother's finger], and says, "Uh oh!" looking at the blocks that fell.

The mother says, "Ouch! My finger!"

Tamara looks at her mother who is shaking her finger.

The mother says, "You stepped on my finger! You gave Mommy a booboo."

Tamara looks stricken, and softly says, "Booboo" looking at the finger.

The mother says, "What are we going to do about it?"

Tamara says, "Kiss booboo," and she does.

The mother hugs Tamara, and says "Oh thank you. It's all better now."

Tamara repeats, "All better now."

● The explanation. . . .

> Tamara says, "Where block?" as she looks around for
> another block on the floor. She is standing since the
> tower they are building is so tall.
> Guessing what Tamara meant, the mother says,
> "Where's another block?" Tamara is not watching the
> mother's face since she is still searching for blocks.
> Tamara says, "'Nother block?"

The mother is expanding Tamara's utterance in her question as
she attempts to clarify her meaning and confirm her guess at
what Tamara meant. This type of adult response/question is an
especially important one to use in connection with expecting that
the child will understand without having to look at the speaker's
face. The child is likely to be motivated to attend to the mother's
utterance since the mother is not introducing new concepts or
topics. Instead she is using the child's topic, showing her interest
in clarifying her meaning, and adding only a small amount of
relevant information to her original utterance. Clarification
questions and expansions were described in Chapters 3 and 4
as being strategies parents use which are likely to promote the
child's language growth. They are also likely to promote the
child's listening. In this instance, Tamara was not looking at the
mother's face when the mother spoke. The fact that she then
imitated the mother's question, employing the mother's word
"another," suggests that Tamara did get the mother's message
through listening alone.

> Mother says, "Hmmm—well, let's see." Mother looks
> for more blocks; Tamara turn away. "Oh—here's one."
> Tamara turns back, and the mother hands her a block.

The mother actually contrived this listening opportunity. That
is, she waited until Tamara had turned away to say "Oh—here's
one."

> The mother then says, "Thank you."
> Tamara says, "What?" and looks at her mother.

Here, Tamara detected the voice, but did not understand what was said.

> **The mother rubs her nose, partially obscuring her mouth, and says, "You can say 'Thank you.'"**
> **Tamara again says, "What?"**

> **This time the mother lets Tamara look at her face as she says, "You're supposed to say 'Thank you.'"**
> **Tamara repeats, "Thank you."**

> **Tamara puts the block on the top of the teetering tower, which then topples. She steps back [right on the mother's finger], and says, "Uh oh!" looking at the blocks that fell.**

In instances where it is desirable to insist on auditory-only input, and the child is looking directly at the adult, there are a number of strategies one can employ. The most obvious is for the speaker to cover his or her own mouth or to otherwise obscure the child's visual access to the mouth. Less obvious is directing the child's visual attention away from the face. Here the mother could have gestured to the block and said, "Look, Mommy gave you a block." When the child's gaze went to the block, she would then say, "You're supposed to say 'Thank you.'" In many instances, it is possible to simply sit behind or beside the child in such a way as to discourage the child from constantly watching the face. After two attempts to give the message auditorally only, the mother let Tamara look at her face as she spoke. There is much controversy regarding how long one should "stay auditory," but in everyday situations, the most reasonable course may be to stay auditory as long as it is possible without destroying the conversational flow or unduly frustrating either adult or child.

> **The mother says, "Ouch! My finger!"**

> **Tamara looks at her mother who is shaking her finger. The mother says, "You stepped on my finger! You gave Mommy a booboo."**

> **Tamara looks stricken, and softly says, "Booboo." looking at the finger.**

> **The mother says, "What are we going to do about it?"**

Tamara says, "Kiss booboo." and she does.

The mother hugs Tamara, and says, "Oh thank you. It's all better now."

Tamara repeats, "All better now."

Tamara turned to the mother's loud "Ouch!" The mother shook her finger because it hurt, but that also meant Tamara looked at the finger while the mother said, "You gave Mommy a booboo." Thus Tamara's repeating of "Booboo" is likely to be based on her having actually heard what her mother said. In hugging Tamara, the mother deprived her of visual access to her face. Tamara's imitation of "All better now" confirms that she heard and listened to her mother's utterance.

In a normal, everyday event such as the second one illustrated here, a general *motivation to listen* is assumed to have been established already; although every instance of listening and understanding is likely to build upon that motivation. *Selective attention* is operating as the child is listening in a normally noisy environment (block play); *localizing* is not much of an issue at the moment since the mother is the only other speaker. Each instance of the child's having understood when she was given access only to the auditory part of the message [through the techniques described above] is an instance of the child using her abilities to *discriminate, identify (categorize, associate)*, as well as to *integrate (interpret, comprehend)*. This example will have been successful if it also illustrates why and how these higher level processes are all "of a piece" in real-life instances, as well as why and how they are inseparable from the child's overall cognitive and linguistic development and abilities.

In any case, the structure and knowledge of the importance of the child's ability to demonstrate the auditory abilities probably needs to be more in the mind of the teacher or parent and generally not particularly obvious in the activities occurring with the child (Boothroyd, 1978). Pollack (1985) says that the hearing-impaired child's auditory abilities develop "because emphasis is placed on listening throughout [all the child's] waking hours so that hearing becomes an integral part of [his or her] personality" (p. 159). Similarly, Ling (1986) says that "learning to listen occurs only when children seek to extract meaning from the acoustic events surrounding them all day and every day" (p. 24). At the same time, as mentioned above, for certain hear-

ing-impaired children, some structured practice on component parts
may be useful as a supplement to the emphasis on audition in normal,
everyday activities. With very young children this structured work will
normally be done through games which, from the child's point of
view, are meaningful and enjoyable. Excellent activities of this sort
are detailed in a number of sources which the reader is strongly
encouraged to consult (Beebe, Pearson, and Koch, 1984; Northcott,
1977, 1978; Pollack, 1985; Vaughn, 1981; Sitnick et al., 1977). With
regard to these more structured activities, however, it is important to
close the chapter by reiterating two themes:

1. The skills or abilities being worked upon are theoretical constructs; consequently, the specific exercises may be somewhat
   arbitrarily-derived; and,

2. Whenever the child learns to perform any task in a structured
   activity or game, it must then be integrated into real-life situations in order to be functional for him or her. That is, provision
   must be made for allowing, encouraging, and expecting the child
   to demonstrate the same ability in the course of normal everyday
   events and activities. Clearly, the more similar to everyday life
   that a adult-planned activity is, the greater the likelihood that
   the child will automatically carry over what has been taught to
   everyday life events.

6
Implementing Intervention

In the final analysis it is not what you do for (hearing-impaired) children (or their parents), but what you have taught them to do for themselves that will make them successful human beings.
(Ann Landers, mildly paraphrased)

Aural habilitation can be viewed as having two types of agendas to address. One is the **affect** agenda that is concerned with the tangle of feelings that can becloud the daily existence of families who are confronted with an event such as hearing impairment in a child. The other agenda is the **content** agenda. This includes information the parents need to absorb about topics such as the nature and implications of hearing loss; the functioning, benefits, and maintenance of hearing aids and other amplification systems; educational choices, and child advocacy; and the development of intelligible spoken language. It also includes strategies or behaviors the parents need to internalize (many of which they may already naturally do) about ways of interacting in order to promote the child's use of audition, and the child's acquisition of intelligible spoken language. These two major agendas, and some suggestions for how to approach or respond to them will be discussed in turn. The emphasis here is not on how the professional works with the child. It is, rather, on how the professional helps the parents or other caregivers accomplish what is needed for the child. "Parents" here is used in a generic sense and includes any and all persons associated with the child's well-being or caregiving. This can mean babysitters, grandparents, older siblings, and other relatives.

In its most enlightened and efficacious form, aural habilitation is a collaborative process between parents and professionals. As Luterman (1984) says, "Parents and professionals are natural allies. They both want in most ardent terms the same thing: a better-communicating child" (p. 157). The efficacy of intervention which views the parent as the primary client has long been supported by research, (See the review in McDade and Varnedoe, 1987), as well as by logical arguments regarding the amount of parent contact with the child, and consequent opportunities for continuity and generalization (Bricker and Casuso, 1979; Ling and Ling, 1978; Northcott, 1977). The discussion that follows concerns affect and content agendas in intervention for very young hearing-impaired children where the parent is considered to be the primary agent of change.

The Affect Agenda

It is generally agreed that the discovery of hearing impairment in one's child is a crisis, or can create one, for the parents and family. The child is just as he or she was the day before, but much is changed for the parents. For a *minority* of parents, it is a relatively small crisis, and the parent can rapidly and relatively smoothly accept the child's hearing loss, and become implicated in the habilitation process. For the vast *majority*, however, the child's hearing loss is first experienced as a catastrophe. Later, the presence and implications of the hearing loss become a simmering crisis which can be coped with, but which periodically returns to an acutely painful stage. Re-eruptions of the emotional crisis often coincide with events such as audiological testing times; with educational transitions into preschool, kindergarten, grade school, or high school; with graduations; with puberty; at young adulthood; and/or at the parent's retirement (Moses and Van Hecke-Wulatin, 1981). These events sometimes precipitate a reworking of the feelings surrounding the continuing implications of the child's hearing loss.

The emotional turmoil surrounding the discovery and presence of hearing loss in a child has been likened to grieving, not unlike the process described by Kubler-Ross (1969). Moses and Van Hecke-Wulatin (1981) have written an excellent chapter which applies grieving process theory to hearing impairment. What is being grieved by the parents is the loss of their dreams and fantasies about what the child would be like. Both prior to and after the child's birth, parents have dreams and expectations for the child's future, most of which require an unimpaired child. When those dreams are shattered by the diagnosis of hearing loss, the parent needs to have a chance to grieve about the situation, to separate from the dreams and to let them go. In the process, grieving may stimulate a re-evaluation of a number of aspects of one's existence including social, emotional, environmental, and philosophic attitudes and beliefs. For example, this may include unconscious biases the parent has toward handicapped people such as fear, pity, or revulsion. Or, it may involve a strong desire for things to remain as they were, a fear of change.

According to Luterman (1984), this process may be an existential "boundary experience" which may force the parent into a more intense awareness of reality and of the transitory nature of existence. The consequence may ultimately be a rearrangement of priorities, an abandonment of trivialities and timidity, and the selection of a different set of meanings for one's existence. Again, though, this is not to imply that one embarks on a linear journey through suffering to a final nirvana of acceptance, coping, and purpose. Being able to accept the situation enough to cope with it and move on does not signal a magical end to the recurrence of painful feelings, nor to the need to work and rework the surrounding issues.

Moses and Van Hecke-Wulatin (1981) include the following emotional states as part of the parental grieving process. These occur in no specific order, or even necessarily by themselves—even though writing requires that they appear so:

> **Denial**—The denial may be of the diagnosis, of the permanence of the hearing loss, and/or of the impact of the hearing loss on the child's life or on the lives of those around him or her.

> **Guilt**—The parents may feel guilt because they believe they caused the hearing loss. Or, they may believe they are being punished for being "bad," or for something they did in the past.

Depression—The parents may feel impotent at not being able to cure the hearing loss. They may be enraged at themselves for not having been able to prevent the loss to start with. They may also feel incompetent to deal with what is seen as the impossible demands being imposed by the hearing loss.

Anger—Anger may be felt by the parents at the injustice of it all. They may also be angry at the unasked-for demands on their time, energy, finances, and emotions. The demands all emanate from the hearing-impaired child, but their anger is often displaced to other family members and to professionals.

Anxiety—Parents may feel anxious from juggling the added pressures and overwhelming responsibilities of having a hearing-impaired child with the need and the right to have an independent life of their own.

These feelings are natural, normal, and perhaps even necessary in order for the parent to deal with the situation and to move on. Each of the emotional states serves a function which eventually allows the parent to separate from their shattered dreams for their "perfect" child and for themselves as the parents of a "perfect" child. Then new dreams can be generated, incorporating the child's hearing impairment. The parent begins to feel that coping is, at least occasionally, possible. The reader is strongly urged to seek out Moses and Van Hecke-Wulatin's excellent article (1981) for further explanation and illustration of the purposes served by each of the emotional states.

So what is the aural habilitation professional supposed to do with all of this emotional turmoil? On a practical level, the turmoil may occasionally get expressed in a "pure" form with a parent so upset that they cannot function at a given moment. Or it may get expressed in a slightly more subtle form such as combinations of alarm, sadness, and frustration about their baby having to receive therapy to learn things other babies learn naturally, about having to learn a lot about something they never wanted to learn about in the first place, about having to participate actively in sessions, about having too many or too few sessions, and/or about the difficulty of finding a parking space near the clinic or school. According to Klevans (1988), Luterman (1979, 1984), Moses (1979, 1985), Moses and Van Hecke-Wulatin (1981), Murphy (1976), Rogers (1951), and Webster (1977), the most facilitative thing the aural habilitationist can do is to convey an attitude of acceptance of whatever the parents' emotional states happen to be.

This is one obvious time when the professional's interpersonal skills will be drawn upon. The idea is not to become a psychotherapist. Indeed, one of the essential aspects of intervention with families of hearing-impaired children is to know when the parents' emotional needs exceed the aural habilitationist's skills, and to refer the parents elsewhere for professional counseling. However, it is not practical, possible, or desirable to refer all upset parents for psychiatric care. The aural habilitationist must accept counseling as a part of his or her professional responsibilities (McWilliams, 1976).

In the vast majority of instances, what is required is direct, honest, and personal confirmation of the other person's "normalness" and "humanness" (Murphy, 1976). This means being genuinely empathic and conveying that intent through active listening. Pickering (1987) calls it "listening as a *receiver* rather than as a critic;" accepting rather than evaluating and trying to control (p. 217). Based on Pickering (1987), Tables 6-1 and 6-2 list and illustrate two general types of responses that the aural habilitationist can make in encounters with parents. Responses that reflect empathy are those which acknowledge and attempt to understand the feelings, perceptions, and interpretations of the parent. These responses increase the parent's feelings of autonomy and self-efficacy. They ultimately have a "freeing" effect. The others, the controlling responses, have a diametrically opposed effect: that of diminishing the parent's feelings of autonomy and self worth. The result of a professional's (even unconscious) attempts to control parents in this way may be either parental resistance (Lowy, 1983), or an overdependence upon the aural habilitationist. The preferred manner of interacting is obvious.

It is through the acceptance and personal confirmation of significant others that the parent may be able to constructively cope with the emotional impact of the child's hearing impairment. The professionals involved may have a powerful impact on the parents in this regard, but this support may also come from friends, religious groups, community and/or parent groups. Parental coping will strengthen the parents' feeling of competence and, in turn, positively affect the child's development.

Feelings will unavoidably come up in aural habilitation sessions with individual parents and their children, so the aural habilitationist must be prepared to address them. However, parent groups can be another extremely valuable and supportive setting. The group can provide

Table 6–1:   Empathic Responses (in Encounters of the Interpersonal Kind).

- Reflecting back what was heard, restating, paraphrasing. (e.g. If I heard you correctly, you said . . . . ?

- Extending, clarifying what the other said. (e.g. Then? And? Tell me more about that. Give me an example. I didn't understand that. What did you mean when you said . . . . ?)

- Using supportive, open-ended, exploratory questions—as nonthreatening as possible! (e.g. What happened to make you feel that way? What do you think of when you hear . . . . ?)

- Summarizing, synthesizing, focusing the other's comments. (e.g. Let me see if I got that: First, he . . . . Then you . . . . Then he . . . .)

- Perception checking. (e.g. Does this fit with the way you see things?)

- Giving feedback on solicited, agreed-upon topics. This can be observable behaviors or one's perceptions of the other's ideas or feelings. If the one receiving feedback is allowed first to discuss his or her own performance and feelings about it, it may save time, and the discussion may be more meaningful. Resources and strengths need to be mentioned; maybe more so than limits and weaknesses, even.

- Acknowledging, without taking the conversation in a different direction. (e.g. Um-hmmm. I see what you mean. I can appreciate what you went through.)

- Encouraging expression of an idea or feeling. (e.g. How did you feel about that?)

- Being quiet.

mutual support in a way that the aural habilitationist cannot. The parents may gain hope, relief, and a feeling of cohesiveness with the other parents. The reader is referred to Luterman (1979, 1984) for in-depth and eloquent treatment of this topic.

Intervention for the child should not be delayed until the parent reaches some mythical level of perfect coping, however. Hearing aids

Table 6–2: **Responses Which Control (in Encounters of the Interpersonal Kind).**

- Changing or diverting the subject without explanation, particularly to avoid discussing the other person's feelings.

- Interpreting, explaining, or diagnosing the other person's behavior. (e.g. You do that because . . . .)

- Giving advice, insisting, or trying to persuade. (e.g. What you should do is . . . .)

- Agreeing vigorously. This binds the other person to their present position.

- Expressing own expectations for the other person's behavior. This type of response can bind the other to the past (e.g. You never did *that* before!), or to the future (e.g. I'm sure you will . . . .).

- Denying the existence or importance of the other's feelings. (e.g. You don't really mean that! You have no reason to feel that way. Everybody has feelings like that.)

- Praising the other for thinking, feeling, or acting in ways you want him or her to; approving on your own personal grounds.

- Judging, disapproving, admonishing on your own personal grounds; blaming, censuring the other for thinking, feeling in ways you do not approve of; imputing unworthy motives.

- Commanding, ordering. (This includes "Tell me what to do!")

- Labelling, generalizing. (e.g. She's always shy. He's aggressive and hyperactive.)

- Controlling through arousing feelings of shame and inferiority. (e.g. How can you do this to me when I have done so much for you?)

- Giving false hope or inappropriate reassurance. (e.g. It's not as bad as it seems.)

- Focusing inappropriately on yourself. (e.g. When my dog died, I felt terrible, too.)

- Probing aggressively, interrogating, asking threatening questions. (Tell me how you think a child learns language.)

must be immediately selected, fitted, worn, and maintained. Children must be exposed to spoken language, and expected to listen, and vocalize or verbalize—as well as to conform to behavioral expectations. The point is that as the content agenda unfolds, the aural habilitationist is dealing with the parent sensitively and empathically, without rejecting, denying, or judging how the parents are feeling or behaving. Fortunately, the child's progress is often one of the most effective catalysts for giant leaps in the parents' ability to cope with it all.

The Content Agenda

The content agenda for parents includes both the absorption of new information and the internalization of strategies for promoting the child's acquisition of intelligible spoken language. Both are vitally important to the child's progress. A number of other recent resources provide a wealth of varied information relevant to work in both of the areas. These include Clark, 1989; Cole and Gregory, 1986; Fey, 1986; Fitzgerald and Fischer, 1987; Hasenstab and Horner, 1982; Ling, 1986, 1989; Pollack, 1985; Schuyler and Rushmer, 1987. All help to provide the sort of information parents need to acquire about hearing loss, amplification, educational choices, child advocacy, and language development. These sources also treat basic principles of sound educational practice such as individualizing instruction, assessing needs, and evaluating progress. In contrast, the focus in this chapter is on what the aural habilitationist can do to help the parent promote the child's learning of intelligible spoken language.

"What the aural habilitationist and parent can do" has two components of paramount importance. These are: (1) Proper selection and maintenance of the child's hearing aids; and (2) the provision of an abundance of appropriate verbal interacting in the course of normal, everyday events. Assuming that the child's hearing aids have been properly selected, and are being carefully monitored and maintained, most of the professional and parent effort can then be directed toward providing the second component: abundant and appropriate communicative experience.

Providing abundant communicative experience is not an especially easy task. There are no universal cookbooks or surefire formulas or even particular language, auditory, or speech-training exercises or activities to be uniformly applied in order to guarantee an outcome of a perfectly intelligible, independent, socialized, and imminently "integratable" child. In fact, in intervention with very young hearing-impaired children, there is no clear separation among language, auditory, and speech work. Any interactive event necessarily taps and exercises all three areas to some degree. What can be done is to be aware of the existence and importance of the synergism of language, auditory, and speech elements to which the child is being exposed in any routine event, and to emphasize them, provide another example, push it all just one more step, make certain the event occurs again, and most of all reinforce and encourage the child by keeping it all meaningful and fun.

This section begins with a discussion of the types of routine, normal, everyday events which provide contexts for language learning. Attention then turns to procedures for examining those normal, everyday events with parents in order to determine areas in the parent's usual interactive behavior which may be facilitating or hindering the child's language growth. This is followed by discussion of ways of emphasizing particular language, auditory, or speech elements in the course of normal, but slightly "embellished," interacting.

Contexts for Communicating

Hearing-impaired children learn language most effectively in the course of normal, everyday events, as do normally hearing children. The essential difference is that for hearing-impaired children, it is important to maintain an *optimally* rich environment or to "embellish" a normal one, as discussed in Chapter 2. Verbal interaction in such an environment must occur consistently, consciously, and frequently in order to establish a desirable level of support.

In this regard, then, much of the job of the aural habilitationist is to heighten the parent's awareness of how much they are already naturally doing, and to encourage them to do more of it. As Clark (1989) says, "The simple routines of everyday life . . . are probably the greatest resource that parents can tap in relation to the developing language of a hearing-impaired child" (p. 47). Particularly in the birth- to two-year-old period, the necessities of household functioning (including especially baby care) work to support the establishment of regular routines. Since these are frequently repeated, the child is provided with nearly the same meaningful experiences with nearly the same language over and over. Examples of routines follow for each of the age/stages detailed in Chapter 5.

Birth to Six Months:

Feeding, getting diapers changed, having baths, getting dressed; getting put to sleep; manipulating simple toys and objects; watching parents, siblings, pets; being fastened into strollers, car seats, infant seats; being engaged in visual/vocal games with adults and siblings (including Peek-a-Boo games).

Six to Twelve Months:

Feeding, getting diapers changed, having baths, getting dressed; being put to sleep; being engaged in simple nursery rhymes involving manipulation of the child and, often, anticipation of tickling, such as "This Little Piggy," "Round and Round the Garden," "Pattycake;" being watched and helped as gross motor skills improve and the child crawls (both on the floor and up the stairs), stands, takes a few steps; being fastened into strollers, car seats, infant seats; taking walks and observing the world; increasingly active play with objects and toys (banging, dropping, throwing, turning, pulling, squeezing); verbal greeting routines, animal sound imitation.

Twelve to Eighteen Months:

Feeding, getting diapers changed, having baths, getting dressed; being put to bed; playing with balls, active motoric play (climbing, bouncing, walking, running); container play (filling and pouring, especially), block play, picture books and stories; drawing with crayons.

Eighteen to Twenty-four Months:

Feeding, getting diapers changed, using the potty (some), having baths, getting dressed, going to bed; active motoric play; play with balls, water, sand, blocks, play dough, crayons; picture books and stories; "helping" with bed-making, dusting, setting the table, sweeping, filling and emptying the dishwasher, cooking, shopping; going to the park; playing on playground toys; nursery rhymes and songs.

Twenty-four to Thirty-six Months:

The same as eighteen to twenty-four months, but with an ever-widening variety of activities.

All of these are contexts for normal, everyday interacting and language "input." The basic idea is to respond to the child's communicative attempts, and to talk about whatever is likely to be of interest to the child about the events or materials at hand. The idea is **NOT** to intrude into the child's self-absorbed exploratory play in order to engage him or her in talk every waking minute, but to select (or create) opportune moments for verbal interaction. This may be through observing the child carefully, and joining in when the child looks up and appears interested in having the parent's involvement. Or, it may be at a moment when the parent has something genuinely exciting, interesting, or important to tell the child about. For some parents, these are already natural behaviors. For others, the notions are easily internalized and expanded upon. For still others, who may be less experienced or less talkative with young children, more guidance and conscious behavior change may be required. For many parents, the Checklist for Caregivers (Chapter 3) can be used to discover how better to facilitate communication, and to initiate changes in interactive behaviors.

Procedures for Using the Checklist for Caregivers

The Checklist described in Chapter 3 outlines caregiver behaviors which have been identified as facilitating communication in the course of everyday interaction. The aural habilitationist will need to decide according to individual cases, whether to discuss the Checklist with the parent as soon as a videotape is made, or to delay discussion of it until it has been privately studied. It may sometimes be wise to select particular aspects of a videotape to discuss (with or without the Checklist).

The interpersonal skills of the aural habilitationist are enormously important in the process of discussing something as personal and sensitive as the way a parent interacts with his or her child. For many of the items of the Checklist, teachers and clinicians routinely make, perhaps unconscious, judgments in any case. Having the items there on the Checklist may bring them up for conscious consideration, and thus promote their more candid and open discussion with the caregivers. Some practical suggestions for addressing the items with sensitivity include the following:

1. With the caregiver, the aural habilitationist can purposefully point out examples of instances on the videotape where the

parent *does* demonstrate a desired behavior. (These can actually be tabulated, if it seems useful to demonstrate a point.) Together, the aural habilitationist and the parent note the effect that the parent's behavior has on the child.

2. The aural habilitationist can simply indicate the next item on the Checklist, and ask the parent if he or she feels it is a problematic one for them.

3. The aural habilitationist can check his or her perceptions with those of the parent. "I don't see a great deal of X in this little segment we videotaped. Is that what happens other times too?" or, "It looks to me as if you are working very hard to get Johnny's attention. Does it seem that way to you, too?"

4. As part of discussing a particular event or item, the aural habilitationist can ask open-ended, exploratory questions concerning that item. Examples might be, "How do you think you (or the child) were feeling at that point?" or, "What happened to make that happen right there?" or, "How does Johnny usually react when you do X ?" These questions can be very tricky to phrase, so that they are not perceived as threatening or critical.

The Checklist provides a guideline for desirable caregiver behaviors. It can be used to help parents become aware of how much they are already doing. It can also be used to identify behaviors they wish to change. In this regard, Luterman's words are relevant when he says, "People will learn just what they are ready to learn and absorb. The best indication of readiness is the question: gratuitous information usually serves to increase confusion and is rarely helpful" (1984, p. 65). Similarly, behaviors the parents themselves identify as problematic are most likely to be the ones about which they will be ready to absorb suggestions. This does not mean that the aural habilitationist has to wait until the parent discovers every problem before bringing it up, but it does mean that the targets will not meet with much success if they are summarily selected and imposed by the aural habilitationist. A way needs to be found to help the parent discover the problematic areas in such a manner that they can "hear" the suggestions for change. The reader is referred to the literature on supervisory relationships (Crago, 1987; Pickering, 1987) for additional related reading on this topic.

Once targets for change have been identified, the next step is to determine how the targets will be worked on. Clearly, this is another instance of something which is most likely to be effective if it comes from the parent, rather than being imposed by the aural habilitationist. But the aural habilitationist needs to be ready with suggestions to offer for the parent's consideration, if there is a need. Methods of achieving adult behavior change vary widely depending upon the behaviors and the individuals involved. Simply becoming aware of the importance of a particular behavior (perhaps as a result of using the Checklist) may be enough to cause a change in some behaviors. After discussion, the parent may just decide to try to keep her voice pitch lower, and do it, for example. Or, the parent may have a means for helping him or herself to make the change. For example, the parent may decide to leave an audiotape recorder running as she is playing with the child at home in order to remind herself to keep her pitch down, and to provide a check of how well she is doing in that regard. Another idea is for the parent to ask someone at home to provide reminders or feedback regarding the behavior—including particularly instances where the change has occurred!

Other behaviors may be more easily changed initially if there is a period of intense feedback from the aural habilitationist. One way to do this is to examine in detail one or more instances where the behavior was problematic on the videotape. This examination might include consideration (primarily by the parent, guided by the aural habilitationist's exploratory questions and "freeing" responses) of what was happening just before the parent behavior occurred, exactly what the parent did, what the parent intended to accomplish by the action, and what effect the parent's behavior had on the child. Then a number of possible alternate behaviors for that instance could be generated. This intensive feedback can be extended into an on-the-spot coaching event, also. This occurs when the parent and child play at some normal activity, and the aural habilitationist quietly interjects a suggestion at the exact moment the behavior either is or is not occurring. Using an FM system for this activity may be a good idea with some parents, assuming there is a one-way mirror arrangement so that the aural habilitationist can be coaching from outside of the room. This kind of intense feedback may be useful for many of the behaviors on the Checklist, but to be effective it must be done with the parent's full agreement.

Probably the most common strategy used in intervention settings is that of "expert" demonstration. The parent is expected to learn how to behave in a certain way from observing the expert do it. In some instances, demonstration can be quite effective, but it does have several inherent dangers. For example, the demonstration may leave the parent feeling overwhelmed and inadequate. It may also have looked so smooth and easy, and occurred so quickly that the parent may have missed the essential point of the demonstration. In order to counteract these possibilities, it may be useful to have the parent take over in interacting with the child immediately after the demonstration, and attempt to replicate it or to perform the desired behavior at the next opportunity.

The possible ways of helping a parent change behaviors are limited only by the particular behaviors involved and by the creativity of the parent and aural habilitationist. The key element in all of this, however, is that the effectiveness of any behavior change plan is directly dependent upon the parent's commitment to it. Lowy (1983) says that adults respond most favorably when they are actively involved in designing and implementing their own learning. This is the reason that it needs to be the parent who recognizes the problematic nature of the behavior, and who generates and enacts the plans for change. It is also the reason that the aural habilitationist needs to interact with the parent in ways which contribute to the *parent's* feeling of autonomy, confidence, and competence.

Strategies for Specific Language, Auditory, and Speech Targets

These sections about work on specific language, auditory, and speech targets may be what some readers were looking for when they picked up this book. If so, and for those who skipped straight to this section, please bear the following in mind:

1. The two components of paramount importance in the interventive treatment of very young hearing-impaired children are properly selected and maintained hearing aids and an abundance of appropriate verbal interaction in the course of normal, everyday events.

2. There is no research evidence supporting the use of any single technique, nor supporting conscious, direct teaching of specific language, auditory, or speech features to hearing-impaired children between the ages of birth and three years.

Ling (1989) makes an interesting differentiation among informal and formal learning, and informal and formal teaching. It is the latter that is of primary concern here. Informal teaching is the "by-product of an apparently unrelated activity," accomplished without deliberate attention being given to it (p. 188). In contrast, formal learning or teaching is seeking after specific goals deliberately, directly, and methodically. It is clear that nearly all of what the birth- to three-year-old child (normally hearing or hearing-impaired) learns, he learns informally. And much of what the parent or professional does with a young hearing-impaired child is clearly informal teaching. For example, the following is an informal teaching event.

The parent and child take a walk after an early summer rain shower, and they come upon a live worm on the sidewalk. The child points it out, "Look! Worm!" The parent replies, "Yes—I see it. Look! The worm is wiggling!" Just in doing this much, the parent is informally teaching the child that what he or she says is meaningful and of communicative value to the parent; that people respond to each other in conversations; that the responding is generally related to the semantic content of the previous speaker's utterance; that the "Mover" [the worm] can perform an [intransitive] "Action;" that the "Mover/Subject" is mentioned first, and then the "Action/Verb;" that the presently occurring action is coded by the use of a present progressive form of *Be* + Verb-*ing*; that the subject is preceded by a definite article *the* that signals that the noun *worm* that follows it is known to both conversational partners. The event is, furthermore, an auditory one, since the parent squatted down to within about eighteen inches of the child's hearing aids, and since the child was looking at the worm as they were talking, not at the parent's face. With regard to informal speech-teaching in this event, the parent's intonation was animated and naturally varied, and thus provided auditory exposure to a normal speech pattern. There were no phonemes being particularly emphasized in the parent's utterance, unless one counts the /w/ since it was used in two words. However, anytime the parent uses spoken language with the child, the child is being informally taught phonemes simply through exposure. All of these teaching aspects of the event can be considered to be by-products of the unrelated wormfinding event, and thus fit the definition of informal teaching.

After having spoken, the parent realizes that the child probably does not know the word "wiggling." On-the-spot, the parent decides it is probably a useful word for this particular child to learn because "wiggling" is an action likely to continue to catch the child's fancy in a number of everyday contexts (worms, strings, spaghetti, the child—all wiggle). So, in the next breath, the parent says, "Wiggle, wiggle, wiggle. The worm is *still* wiggling!" (pause for the child to respond) "Oh look! There's another worm that's wiggling." (pause —The child finds a third worm.) "Oh—you found another one! Is that worm wiggling?" (pause) "Yes, it is! Oh, that's funny. Can you wiggle like a worm?" And so on. In the parent's mind, "wiggle" has become a vocabulary goal. The parent is deliberately providing varied, repetitive exposure to that goal, and attempting to elicit it. In terms of Ling's differentiation, the event is now somewhere between an informal and a formal one. The goal is specific and deliberately sought-after, and the adult's actions are intended to reduce the time period required for the child to learn the word through depending entirely on the vagaries of totally natural exposure. For those reasons, the event could be considered to be a formal teaching event. However, the teaching is informal in that it is occurring with the child and parent focussed on a normal everyday activity, and the adult is employing ordinary language appropriate to that event (taking a walk and finding a worm).

A resolution to this definitional dilemma is to describe the adult's on-the-spot activity as an "embellished" informal teaching event. This is another variation on the theme (in Chapter 2) that what is needed in order to provide a hearing-impaired child with optimal auditory and linguistic stimulation are embellishments of the normal situation. The focus of much of what follows regarding intervention with specific language, auditory, and speech aims is **embellished informal teaching**.

Embellished Informal Teaching of Language, Listening and Speech

Language

The *Checklist for Caregivers* is at the heart of the spoken language intervention approach in this book. The fundamental objectives are for the caregiver to make every effort to create a positive, accepting, and interesting communicative environment, and to interact with the child in ways that will promote the child's motivation to communicate verbally with increasing effectiveness. All of the items of the Checklist relate to those objectives.

Underlying informal teaching embellishments that can be used to facilitate the child's learning of specific aspects of language, is an important language-learning principle: the "Informativeness Principle" of Greenfield and Smith (1976). It is somewhat related to Bates' (1976) *given-new* concept. The idea is that, at the one-word stage of linguistic development, when the child is going to talk, he or she is most likely to verbally encode the most informative (interesting, novel, uncertain, dynamic) element of the situation. So, for example, if the child's cookie falls off the table, the most likely utterance will concern the "fell down" business, not the "cookie" part. And if the child says nothing, the preferred adult utterance might be "It fell down," rather than "Oh! The cookie!" Of course, the aspect which is the most informative to the child may not always be obvious and predictable. If the cookie falls off the table and the dog rapidly gobbles it up, one is faced with the quandary of whether "fell down," "all gone," or "doggie!" is the most interesting aspect of the situation to the child.

Fey (1986) amply supports the suggestion that informativeness should be made a basic principle in clinical practice. This means, for example, that in providing the child with the words appropriate to what he or she wants to express, the parent would need to be observing keenly in order to encode the most informative aspect of the situation—which is presumably what the child would be trying to express. (See Checklist items #2, #3, #6, #7, #10, #13.) The Informative Principle also has implications for the use of expansions. Howe's (1981) "extended" expansions (which provide related and new ideas to the child's original utterance) fit well with the concept of informativeness. "Minimal" syntactic expansions fit less well since the addition of a plural "s" or an "-ing" probably has low informativeness value to the child. (See Checklist Item #11.)

Responding with a response which includes a question or comment for the child (Checklist Item #8), will also be most effective if the question or comment is purposefully centered on some salient, novel, or uncertain aspect. If one stretches the principle to include **being** informative, dynamic, and interesting, it could also include speaking in phrases and sentences of appropriate length and complexity, as well as speaking in an interesting and animated voice. (See Checklist Items #16 and #19.)

Several language intervention techniques that are not on the Checklist merit particular mention. They are excellent examples of ways of carrying out embellished informal teaching, and they also adhere to the Informativeness Principle. They can be used to emphasize any language feature(s) that fit with the expectations for that child's age and stage as outlined in Chapter 5. One of the techniques is the use of multiple exemplars as discussed by Fey (1986). When an event occurs where the child has produced a target item or an approximation to it, the parent recreates and repeats the event using materials similar to those of the child. For example, if the child is pretending to make a stuffed bear jump off a chair and says, "Jump!", the adult [immediately thinking either of extended expansions or of Mover-Action, intransitive sentence frames(!)] could then say:

"Yes, the bear jumped right off the chair!" [picking up a stuffed dog]

"And then the doggie jumped." (making dog jump)

"And the kittycat jumped." (making cat toy jump)

"And then the elephant said, 'I want a turn!' (getting the elephant ready to jump, and then pausing)

"So then. . . ."

And hopefully, the child would say something like, "Elephant jump." This provision of multiple exemplars could also be used with a child who is not yet using words. The adult would similarly observe the child's play, provide the words, and vary one aspect of the play in an interesting and fun manner. A variation on the multiple exemplar theme would be to provide several instances of exactly the same event, followed by one different one. Here, the adult would participate in the toy bear jumping off of the chair several times (while talking about it), and then have the bear *climb up* the chair to create a related, but new and remark-worthy event.

Other intervention techniques which conform to the Informativeness Principle require an already established routine between the adult and the child. Consequently, they would not be appropriate with very small infants, and they simply will not work until the child has enough experience with the event to have built up an expectation regarding the way it should go. These strategies are from Constable (1983), based on Lucas' (1980) idea of the adult being a "saboteur" of routine events in order to stimulate communication about them. One way to do this is to violate the order of the steps or to omit one. For example, in making orange juice with the child, the parent could have the child pour the frozen juice into a container, and add the cans of water. Then the adult would act as if he or she was going to pour it into glasses (skipping the step of stirring). Or, object function can be violated through getting ready to pour the juice into a shoe or a hat. As mentioned above, the success of these techniques hinges on the child's knowledge that there is a "right" way for these events to occur. Otherwise, nothing will be said as the child will innocently accept what the adult is doing as normal behavior. But when it works, it can be great fun since any harmless violation of expectations of this sort is likely to evoke laughter.

Other strategies are perhaps more obvious such as hiding objects in order to stimulate "Where?" questions, or to stimulate guesses as to the object's location. (It is not necessary to fake this situation in most households). Another strategy, long recommended by teachers of the deaf, is to require that the child vocalize or speak in order to get something. This operant strategy is probably acceptable for phrases and situations well known to the child, similar to the common "You have to say 'please' before I'll give it to you." phenomenon. But the inherent danger is that it can turn into a power struggle, which the parent never wins no matter what the outcome.

To reiterate, then, the parents' job is to provide an abundance of appropriate verbal interacting in the course of normal, everyday events. Within the course of this normal-but-embellished interacting, there are some strategies which the parent can use to emphasize particular language elements which are appropriate for the child's age and stage. These include providing the child with the words to describe what *the child* is likely to think is the most interesting aspect of the situation; providing extended expansions (rather than minimal ones); using various kinds of multiple exemplar techniques; violating the order of events or the function of objects; and purposefully setting up the environment so that a target is likely to be used (e.g. hiding objects). The notion underlying all of these strategies, as well as underlying the Informativeness Principle, is that language is used for communicating—and all of these strategies create a **reason** to communicate. The possibilities are limited only by one's ingenuity.

Listening (Audition)

Examples in Chapter 5 illustrate the ways in which normal, everyday activities can be embellished in order to provide the child with opportunities to auditorally attend selectively; localize; discriminate;

identify, categorize, associate; integrate, interpret, and comprehend. The suggestion was made that parents need to be aware that these "listening events" are occurring and are important. Then they will be able and motivated to create similar listening opportunities whenever possible in order to enhance the child's automatic and full use of residual hearing.

In the last section of this chapter, there is an example of more formal (semiformal) auditory teaching of language and speech targets. This kind of teaching, which is carefully explained below, may be appropriate for some hearing-impaired children in the latter half of the age period of concern here. For additional activities intended to work on each of the theoretical auditory constructs, the reader is referred to Beebe et al., 1984; Northcott, 1977, 1978; Pollack, 1985; Sitnick et al., 1977; Vaughn, 1981. Strategies which can be employed when it is desirable to insist on auditory-only input (obscuring visual access to the mouth, directing visual attention elsewhere, sitting behind or beside the child) are also described in chapter 5.

Speech

Phonating/Vocalizing

With some exceptions, very young hearing-impaired children are usually vocalizing to some extent at the time that the hearing loss is detected. The task of the parents is to encourage an abundance of vocalizing by the child through consistently and positively responding to it (Ling, 1989). The encouragement often takes the form of the parent smiling, looking interested, moving closer to the child, and imitating the vocalization. The child may also be encouraged to vocalize as a result of hearing and experiencing others talking around him or her. This would include the interactive nonsense babbling that parents sometimes initiate with babies, as well as humming and singing near the child. In fact, simply hearing language spoken to and around him or her may be a motivation to the child to vocalize.

The young hearing-impaired child's voice may sound quite normal. Or, if the child is more than six or eight months of age at detection of a severe-to-profound hearing loss, there may be some voice abnormalities beginning. For example, the vocalizations may be relatively infrequent, the vocal quality may be strained (providing the child with a greater orosensory feedback), the repertoire may be limited (e.g. to central vowels and a few consonants), or the voice may be too loud or too soft. Usually, after the child begins consistently wearing amplification and receiving an abundance of appropriate verbal stimulation, most of these problems begin to ameliorate. That is, the child often starts to vocalize more frequently, with greater variety, and with a better-modulated voice. The length of time this takes varies with the degree of the child's hearing loss, his age of detection (and how well-practiced the vocal habits have become), and the amount and nature of the auditory input. Pollack (1970) suggested the concept of "hearing age" as a guideline for expectations in this regard. The fundamental notion is that, before beginning to talk, a hearing-impaired child with a severe-to-profound hearing loss who has just been provided with appropriate amplification, should be expected to need a "listening time" similar in length to that of a normally hearing child. Normally hearing children often produce their first word(s) after ten to twelve months of listening, and it may help to remind the parents of that when they become discouraged. Northcott (1978) details a variety of speech-related auditory accomplishments and when they can expect to be seen for children with different degrees of hearing loss. An older child who has a longer attention span and/or is especially quick to learn may experience somewhat faster gains in some areas as the learning steps are "collapsed."

If, with the somewhat older child, there are persistent problems with the child's vocal quality or intensity, or if the vocalizations remain very infrequent or limited in variety, it may be useful to employ more formal (semiformal) techniques to elicit and practice the targets. In most cases, the child will need to be at least eighteen to twenty-four months of age in order to cooperate for this type of activity. And, naturally, the practiced targets will need to be put into use in normal conversational situations to become fully acquired. More formal techniques for speech work are described in the final section of this chapter.

Prosodic Features and Segmental Phonemes

Both prosodic features and segmental phonemes can be made more salient through consistently employing particular expressions, words, or sounds in normal routine activities or games. Salience, here, is primarily a matter of repeatedly exposing the child to the targets, while making it fun and exciting so that the child will automatically want to attend. It is also important to leave frequent pregnant pauses to encourage the child's participation. The sought-after child participation in most instances is verbal or vocal imitation, with the child eventually using the expressions, words, or sounds spontaneously in other similar events.

Normally developing children frequently begin to experiment with prosodic elements at about four to six months of age, the stage that Oller (1977, 1980, 1983) labels the Expansion Stage. (See Chapter 4, p 74.) These prosodic features are rudimentary variations in the pitch, intensity, and timing characteristics of the child's early vocalizations. The normal developmental sequence thus provides a justification for prosodic elements being an appropriate "target" for exposure and emphasis early in the intervention process. Acquisition of normal pitch, intensity, and timing characteristics is important for expressing meaning and emotion in conventional ways in spoken language. It is important for marking constituent (thought) boundaries in sentences. Fortunately most of the acoustic cues for prosodic variations occur below 1000 Hz, which means that they are available to most hearing-impaired children.

The vowel repertoire for normally developing children at six to twelve months is predominantly lax central vowels, such as /ɛ , I, æ, ʌ, ʋ/. The phonemes /i/ and /u/ are infrequent right through eighteen months of age. In spite of this, it may make sense to consciously and abundantly expose even the very young hearing-impaired child to words and to toy and animal sounds containing the phonemes /i/ and /u/. The reason for this is related to the fact that these two sounds represent the end points on the vowel continuum [in terms of articulation as well as acoustics]. If the child can learn to produce these end points, as well as central vowels such as /a/, then the remaining vowels can usually be "filled in" as slight adjustments of the /i/, /u/, or the central vowel.

With regard to consonants, normally developing children primarily use stops and nasals at six to twelve months, and add in fricatives between twelve and eighteen months. There is a great deal of variability among children in the particular sounds they produce in their early words, and in the stability of the most frequently observed sounds from one time to the next. Consonants occurring in reduplicated syllables gradually increase in frequency and variety between six and twelve months. However, between seven to ten months, at least half of the vocal productions are vocalizations which are *not* reduplicated (Oller, 1983), so parents and professionals should adjust their expectations accordingly [keeping the "hearing age" notion in mind].

Ling (1989) provides a wealth of strategies for informally developing all aspects of speech. These informal strategies are directly applicable in work with very young hearing-impaired children, and are entirely compatible with the orientation of the present book. After the child imitates speech sounds on demand (by about eighteen to twenty-four months of age), it may be useful and reassuring to the parents to track the child's progress using the Ling *Phonetic Level Evaluation* (PLE) forms. There should be no effort to teach the sounds rigidly according to the order on the form, however. By eighteen to twenty-four months, a particular profoundly hearing-impaired child may be manipulating some suprasegmentals, and gradually increasing the vowel and consonantal repertoires in a manner which may not precisely conform to that on the PLE, which was designed for remedial rather than developmental progression. It would therefore be a mistake to try to force the child's developing repertoire to conform. Nonetheless, the PLE forms can be used to track progress, and studied to determine particular features or sounds that are missing and that could therefore be gainfully made salient in play activities and conversation (or more formal teaching, as described in the final section of this chapter).

One frequently suggested technique for enhancing perception and production of speech sounds is that of associating a selected sound with a particular toy or with a frequently occurring event. Examples follow of sound-toy and sound-event associations that can be used in many daily situations:

Intonation—Use expressions such as "uh oh" [for things falling down], "all gone" [for food being finished; toys rolling under furniture], "oh no!" [for toys colliding or breaking; accidents of all kinds], "wow!" [for delightful events], "mmmm" [for anything smelling or tasting good], /a/ or /ai/ of long duration [to signify flying of airplanes or birds]. Produce the phrases with very marked high/low contrasts of the intonational contours.

Intensity—Use "Shhhh!" and a whisper for any quiet events such as a baby or doll sleeping. Play the "Wake Up" game where one person closes their eyes and pretends to sleep ["Shhhh! *X* is sleeping."]. The other one shouts ["Boo!" or the person's name] to wake them up.

Duration—Use expressions that have interesting contrasts of rhythmic patterns such as "So. . . . big!"; or "Drip drip drip" for a faucet or for rain falling off of a flower; or "mmmm" for something smelling or tasting good; or "up up up up—down. . . ." for a small doll climbing up a slide and then coming down; "Choo-choooo. . . ." for a train.

Vowels—

/a/ hop hop hop [a rabbit or a frog]; hot!

/i/ *peek*-a-boo! or peek! Go to sleep! Whee!

/u/ Boo! mooooooooo [train whistle]

/au/ meow, bowwow, ow! round and round, mouth

/ai/ bye-bye, eye, hi

/ɛ/ bed, wet!

/ʊ/ push, woof woof

/æ/ quack quack, Daddy

/ʌ/ up, cut

/o/ nose, no no! It broke./It's broken.

Consonants—

/b/ bye-bye, boo

/p//pʌp/\pʌ/ [boat sound], pop! [bubbles]

/w/ walk walk walk [any toy or person walking]

/m/ mmmmmm [for something smelling or tasting good]

/h/ hi! hohoho [Santa Claus]

/ʃ/ Shhh

/f/ off! foot

/tʃ/ ch-ch-ch [train sound]

/r/Errrrr [siren sound]

/l/ hello

In order to be effective, the sound must be used consistently whenever the child plays with the toy, or the event occurs. The child can thus learn in a very natural manner to associate the toy or event with both listening for and producing the chosen sound.

Semiformal Auditory Teaching of Language and Speech

According to Ling's (1989) definition, formal teaching involves deliberate, direct, methodical teaching by an adult with particular goals in mind for the learner. The teaching event illustrated in the example which follows certainly has those characteristics. However, the teaching occurs through playful activity. The child's focus remains primarily on the toys and the interplay with the adults, while the goals are accomplished as a by-product of the activity. These latter characteristics are those of informal teaching. The kind of teaching described below seems to require the invention of an additional term: "semiformal" teaching. A continuum of teaching styles could thus be portrayed as follows:

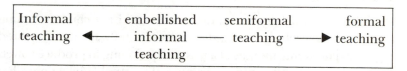

Formal teaching is what happens in traditional educational settings for school-aged children, and is inappropriate for children between the ages of birth and three years. At the other end of the continuum, informal teaching is what happens in normal everyday conversational interaction. Embellished informal teaching occurs when the parent "seizes the moment" to emphasize some auditory, speech, linguistic, or communicative aspect of a normal, everyday event. Semiformal teaching is an adult-directed, preplanned play activity with specific goals and objectives for the child's behavior during the activity. The first two teaching approaches, informal and embellished informal teaching, are employed by parents and professionals with all children. The third, semiformal teaching, is generally employed by a professional and is used only with selected children who are at least eighteen to twenty-four months of age. Although parents may wish to employ elements of semiformal teaching at home, they may find that attempting to recreate activities from therapy sessions in their entirety strains the parent-child relationship, and ends in frustration for all.

It is not until the child is at least eighteen to twenty-four months of age that he or she may be able to and be interested in cooperating in brief speech games and activities which an adult sets up and directs. This type of operant activity can be done with any toy that has pieces (puzzles, play dough pump, Mr. Potato), or any activity that has a repeated movement (stamp pad, stacking blocks, stringing beads, a light appearing in a light box, animal toys coming out of a box or going to sleep in a barn). The idea is that the aural habilitationist controls the toy, pieces, or activity, and the child must produce or imitate a particular speech sound in order to get the next piece or make the next move. It is at this time that there can be much more identifiable auditory and speech work. The aural habilitationist can push for clearer production, or can use this type of activity to elicit new sounds, or to have the child do selection tasks based on auditory discrimination, identification, and/or comprehension. At the same time, the semiformal teaching event is couched in normal and correct language. An example follows:

● The context. . . .

> The aural habilitationist, the mother, and the child are sitting at a small table. This particular profoundly hearing-impaired child of twenty months of age is just beginning to produce vowels with some variety and on demand. The aural habilitationist has three small toys hidden in a box: a rabbit (for /a/ in hop hop hop); a cow (for /u/ in mooo); and a dog (for /au/ in bow wow). The specific speech goals in the aural habilitationist's mind are for the child to imitate /a/, /u/, /au/ in the course of the activity; the auditory goals are to participate in the routines for listening, and to select correctly each toy when its sound is produced. The language goals include learning "hop," "moo," and "bow wow" as lexical items of a sort, as well as more informal goals of being optimally exposed to language and communication.

> The choice of "hop hop hop" and "Moooo!" and "Bow wow!" as three words using the three target phonemes was not random. The three words provide salient contrasts in duration which may be the acoustic parameter that the child first utilizes in discriminating among them. Further, they are all mid-to-low frequency, intense sounds which enhances the likelihood of the child easily detecting them and attending to them. And finally, /au/ is a diphthong requiring rapid tongue movement (always a desirable target) from the /a/-part to the /u/-part of the diphthong.

N.B. In the interests of space conservation, this semiformal teaching event will be presented only once (unlike the format in Chapter 6 where the events were shorter). Sections which are discussed directly following the example have been marked with upper case letters which correspond to the appropriate comments.

● The action. . . .

(A)

The aural habilitationist shakes the box, looking intrigued, and says, "I hear something. I think there's something in the box.... Listen, Mommy!" The aural habilitationist hands the box to the child's mother.

The mother also shakes the box, looks interested and curious, and says, "I hear something too! Here, Alan—you want to listen too?" She hands the box to the child.

Alan shakes the box with vigor, vocalizing with a central vowel sound he frequently uses.

The mother smiles and says, "You hear that too, don't you!"

(B)

Alan starts to try to open the box. The box is purposely fastened in such a way that a child cannot open it. Alan hands the box to the aural habilitationist, looks her in the eye, and vocalizes.

(C)

The aural habilitationist accepts the box and says, "Oh, okay. You want me to open the box. Here, I'll open it for you." The aural habilitationist quickly removes the rabbit from the box and conceals it in her hand. She says, "I found a little bunny rabbit! This rabbit goes 'hop hop hop.'" As she says "hop hop hop," she brings up her hand holding the rabbit to partially conceal her mouth. She says "hop hop hop" again in this way, and then reaches her hand out (still holding the rabbit) toward the mother's face.

The mother recognizes this as a cue to repeat what the aural habilitationist said and did. The mother immediately says, "The rabbit goes 'hop hop hop'" and makes the rabbit hop. The child's eyes are on the rabbit, not on the mother's lips, so the mother does not try to conceal her mouth.

The aural habilitationist then says, "Yes! It goes 'hop hop hop'" holding the hand-concealed rabbit in front of her mouth again, smiling, and looking pleased. She then reaches it toward the child's mouth, as she had just done with the mother, as a cue for the child to produce (imitate) the sounds. The child says "uh uh uh" / $\wedge$ - $\wedge$ - $\wedge$ / and the aural habilitationist smiles and says, "Yes, that's right. The rabbit goes 'hop hop hop' right over to you!" She gives the rabbit to the child to play with for a few minutes.

(The action to this point has taken about sixty seconds, at most; the child plays with the rabbit for another minute or two.)

(D)

Then the aural habilitationist brings out a toy barn and places it on the table in front of the child. The aural habilitationist says, "Alan, the rabbit is *so* sleepy. He wants to go to sleep. He wants to go to sleep in the barn." She opens the barn door and puts the rabbit inside. The aural habilitationist says, "Night night, rabbit. Go to sleep. Shhhh!" She shuts the barn door, pushes the barn to the far side of the table out of the child's reach, while saying, "Night night, rabbit. Shhhh!" again.

(The going-to-sleep episode takes ten to twenty seconds. It could be more if the child participated a great deal, or if he objected to giving up the toy.)

(E)

This same routine is repeated for the other two toys (the cow and the dog), with the parent being the one who controls the toys, exposes the child to the targets, and attempts to elicit them.

After all three animals are safely sleeping in the barn, the aural habilitationist glides right into an auditory selection activity. While Alan is looking at the barn where the last animal just disappeared, the aural habilitationist can say, "Uh oh. Time to wake up, cow! Can you wake up the cow, Alan? I want the one that goes 'Moooo'! Can you wake up the one that goes 'Moooo'?" Alan looks blankly at the aural habilitationist. The aural habilitationist says, "Let's see if Mommy can help. Mommy, can you get me the one that goes 'Moooo'?"

The mother does, saying "Come on, cow. Wake up. Time to go! Moooo!" The mother puts the cow back in the box the aural habilitationist is holding and says, "Bye-bye cow! Moooo!" The exit of the other animals is similarly handled, with the child being given every opportunity to select the correct toy based on the auditory message alone, as well as to produce the sound. The activity is over when the last animal is inside the box.

[As it is written here, the entire activity requires ten to fifteen minutes.]

- The explanation. . . .

    (A) The box-shaking routine is done to encourage the child to listen and to be curious about sounds he hears. By having the mother listen, and then react to hearing the sound, the aural habilitationist has provided the child with a model of listening, being interested and being excited about listening. Also, by having the parent immediately "take over" and perform the same activity, the aural habilitationist demonstrated an embellished informal strategy for the parent that could be used in other everyday instances. If there were some problem in the parent's ability to carry out the activity, the aural habilitationist could gently coach the parent right at that moment.

(B) The box is "child-proofed" so that the child will be required to ask for help in order to get it open. This creates a need for the child to express a request for an action, and allows exposure to an "Open the _X_ ." routine.

(C) The aural habilitationist's actions are intended to encourage the child to listen to and imitate the 'hop hop hop.' She conceals the rabbit in order to add an element of mystery. She speaks in phrases and sentences of normal length, and uses the 'hop hop hop' target in a sentence, not just in isolation. The aural habilitationist covers her mouth in order to require that the child listen to the target. The hand cue is consciously used in order to signal the moment when the other person is supposed to imitate. The mother is again used as a model for the child's behavior. If the child had not imitated, the mother could have demonstrated 'hop hop hop' again; then the child could be given one more opportunity to produce the target prior to being given the toy. The child needs to be given the toy as a reward for staying involved in the activity, even if he does not produce the sound!

(D) This part of the activity allows the toys to be left on the table, but out of sight, and out of immediate consideration. It also allows for exposure to the routines for "Go to sleep" [for the /i/ sound] and to "Shhhh!" [for the /ʃ/ sound].

(E) The principles are the same in this last section as for the preceding parts. The context is play; the language is normal; the targets are generally incorporated into complete sentences; much repetitive but varied exposure to the targets is provided; at the aural habilitationist's request, the mother demonstrates auditory and speech behaviors for the child; the aural habilitationist demonstrates strategies for the parent to use in order to encourage the child to listen and to imitate; the parent attempts the activities immediately after the aural

habilitationist; and the parent does the majority of the interacting with the child, rather than the aural habilitationist.

About the Structure of Semiformal Teaching Events

Semiformal teaching of this kind usually has three parts to it: (1)
getting the toys or materials out in front of the participants, (2) playing
with the toys or materials, and (3) getting the toys or materials put
away again. Each part of the event has auditory, speech, language,
and management routines associated with it which, once learned by
all the participants, make the event flow smoothly.

The speech and language routines are centered around consistent
use of the sound-toy and sound-event associations. Examples from
the illustration include the box-opening episode *"Open the X ."*, and
the episode where the animals were put to sleep in the barn *"Go to
sleep. Shhhh!"*. One auditory routine in the illustration occurs at the
outset where the box is shaken, making a noise, and the aural habilitationist and the mother model listening behavior while talking about
it. When the aural habilitationist and the mother conceal their mouths,
it is a routine intended to require the child to listen carefully. But it
also could be considered a management routine, whereby the child
is being cued to listen as a preface to being asked to imitate or respond.
Using the mother to model correct responding behavior probably also
provides the same sort of management cue *"Be alert—you are next!"*,
as does the practice of holding a closed hand near the mouth of the
person whose turn it is to speak.

It should be noted that these are **not** routines until the child and
parent have participated in them a number of times!

About the Benefits and/Limitations of
Semiformal Teaching

For the child who cooperates easily in semiformal teaching, there is
likely to be one major benefit: The time period required for the child
to acquire the targets through natural exposure may be reduced. This
may happen because of the amount of repetition provided, and because the demands for imitative practice which occur in a semiformal
teaching event of this kind. For the aural habilitationist who employs
this kind of activity, there may accrue a feeling that tangible progress
is being carefully crafted, and that "real" teaching is going on. The

parent may also feel comfortable with semiformal activities for those reasons.

However, as noted at the beginning of the section on strategies for specific language, auditory, and speech targets, there is no research evidence supporting the use of conscious, direct teaching of specific language, auditory, or speech features to hearing-impaired children between the ages of birth and three years. One of the problems with semiformal teaching of specific targets is that the child's learning may not generalize to other situations, or in the worst case, the targets learned may not even be appropriate for use in situations other than "therapy." This is clearly something to guard against in planning and carrying out semiformal teaching.

Other problems with semiformal teaching stem from the fact that this kind of adult-directed and adult-controlled activity violates several accepted principles of normal communication and of child development. What is being violated (relative to an informal or an embellished informal teaching event) is that the **adult** has selected the activity and the toys to be played with, the **adult** talks first, the **adult** attempts to get the child to perform specific listening and speaking tasks on demand. These are violations to be carefully considered if the intention is to promote the development of a child who spontaneously initiates meaningful communication frequently and creatively, and who has solid feelings of autonomy, independence, and *self*-control. The adult is very much "in charge" of this kind of activity, and the child's primary role is to cooperate by listening, imitating, and doing what he or she is told. For some children, even at five years of age, these are very exacting demands! However, although the period from eighteen months to three years is notorious as a time for children to be asserting their independence through the full variety of noncooperative tactics, a number of young children really enjoy short periods of adult-directed play. The success of this type of activity seems to hinge on the child's desire to comply, and on the teacher's ability to keep the child's interest and enthusiasm high.

Strategies for maintaining the child's interest and enthusiasm are the ones which promote the activity's naturalness and informality. These include playing with vigor and enthusiasm; smiling, patting, and hugging the child; using age-appropriate toys; creating mystery and curiosity (hiding the toys); letting the child be as active as possible (letting the child shake the box, and eventually play with the toys); judging the pace of the steps appropriately (moving quickly from one step to the next, but at the same time pausing to allow the child sufficient time to participate); and recognizing and responding in a positive manner to all of the child's attempts to communicate. These strategies may somewhat mask the adult-directiveness, and make the semiformal teaching event communicative and fun.

The most important thing to remember in implementing intervention intended to help the parent help the child learn to talk, is to **listen to the parent and to the child**. Plans are meant to be carefully prepared, and then tossed rapidly out the window if competencies or interests were improperly estimated, or if other needs arise which are more pressing. Indeed, perhaps B.F.Skinner (1964) provided a proper perspective when he said, "Education is what survives when what has been learned has been forgotten" (p. 484).

7

In A Nutshell: A Summary

A BASIC PREMISE OF THIS BOOK IS THAT MOST HEARING-IMPAIRED CHILDREN CAN LEARN TO LISTEN, UNDERSTAND, AND TALK . . .

This book has carefully examined features of the child's world which are important for helping parents foster listening, understanding, and speaking in their very young hearing-impaired children. In light of recent technological and educational advances, the acquisition of intelligible spoken language is a realistic goal for the majority of hearing-impaired children. However, research and experience have shown us that the hearing-impaired child's acquisition of spoken language can be threatened on a number of fronts. One threat is a political movement afoot whose aim is to remove spoken language acquisition from the spotlight in the education of young hearing-impaired children. Another threat stems from budgetary prioritizing and/or ignorance in many medical centers which continues to result in children's hearing losses being identified late, and the introduction of hearing aids and educational intervention delayed. Still another threat comes from hearing aids being improperly selected, fitted, or maintained. Fortunately there are many notable exceptions to all of these potential roadblocks to the child's learning to talk. However, even when the hearing loss has been identified early and the hearing aids appropriately selected and well-maintained, there can be threats to the child's spoken language learning which arise from the parent being inadequately informed, guided, and supported throughout the often emotional as well as long and arduous process. The aim of this book has been to provide a fresh, reasonable, and research-based framework for professionals who are carrying out early intervention where spoken language development is a major goal, and where the parent or some other close caregiver is seen as the key to the child's learning.

. . . FOLLOWING A NORMAL DEVELOPMENTAL COURSE . . .

Already by the age of three, normally developing children have an impressive degree of communicative competence. That is, as described in Chapters 1 and 2, they have absorbed enough cultural and interpersonal knowledge to make the pragmatic, semantic, syntactic, and phonologic choices that result in their utterances being linguistically and contextually appropriate most of the time. Although we do not know exactly what makes the child progress from one state of knowing to the next, we do know what the important genetic and environmental elements seem to be in order for the process to occur. We also know quite a lot about what the child can do at various points in the process. Until proven otherwise, the aural habilitation professional makes the assumption that all of the child's abilities, of genetic or environmental origin, can be influenced through teaching. The aural habilitationist tries to help the parent create an optimally rich language-learning environment to help compensate for the lack of clarity and redundancy of exposure resulting from the child's hearing loss. Given this kind of optimally rich auditory and linguistic experience, in most cases the child's development can be expected to follow a normal course, although in many cases with some delay.

. . . GIVEN AN EMBELLISHED LANGUAGE-LEARNING AND AUDITORY ENVIRONMENT.

An optimally rich environment for a hearing-impaired child is basically a normal one, with embellishments. The two most important embellishments are: (1) consistent wearing of appropriate, properly maintained hearing aids, and (2) provision for abundant verbal interacting during which the adult behaviors are those which promote the child's listening and spoken language development. Language-promoting caregiver behaviors include being warm, responsive, nurturing, and appropriately stimulating. Further, caregivers of normally developing children modify their talk in ways which have become known as "motherese." The modifications, detailed in Chapter 2, include characteristic choices of topics, speech patterns, reduced complexity, and repetition as well as increased responsiveness and persistent attempts to understand the child. All of these modifications could be at least partly explained as attempts to elicit conversational participation from the child. Other conversational embellishments with the same goal, sometimes employed by caregivers of normally developing children and often employed in intervention situations, include the use of multiple exemplars which introduce moderate novelty within a familiar conversational context, purposeful and playful violation of the order of steps in a process or with the function of objects, and hiding objects or withholding objects in an effort to stimulate talking on the child's part. These are described in Chapter 6. All of these strategies for embellishing the child's language-learning environment are most useful if they are internalized by the parent and automatically used as appropriate in the course of normal, everyday play and caregiving with the child.

In addition to the language-promoting strategies, other strategies need to be simultaneously employed in order to help the child use his or her residual hearing to the greatest extent possible within those same everyday interactive events. Using audition for learning spoken language is the logical and most efficacious approach since, in terms of sensory experience, spoken language is primarily an acoustic (sound-based) event. Auditory processing models have identified a number of component abilities which overlap and interrelate in any sort of conversational or auditory learning activity. These abilities include attending to sound; detecting, localizing, discriminating, identifying sounds; listening selectively; and comprehending auditory input. Clearly, it is possible to emphasize component abilities in isolated auditory training activities. But particularly with very young hearing-impaired children, growth in useful auditory abilities is inextricably linked to cognitive and spoken language growth. Consequently, the most reasonable approach is for the child's caregivers to be aware of the importance of encouraging the child to listen rather than always to watch the speaker's face, and to be aware of the use of the many opportunities and strategies for allowing the child to do so in the course of ordinary events. This is detailed and illustrated with examples in Chapter 5.

CRUCIALLY IMPORTANT FEATURES FOR INTERACTING ARE DETAILED IN THE CHECKLIST FOR CAREGIVERS AND THE ITEM EXPLANATIONS, . . .

The Checklist for Caregivers (Chapter 3) is a compilation of those caregiver behaviors which are believed to foster spoken language learning. Using the Checklist, the interventionist and/or parent can consider the appropriateness of the parent's role in communicative interactions with their child. Features on the Checklist are divided into two sections: those pertaining to the parent's establishment of a warm and positive relationship with the child, and those pertaining to the interactive mechanics of conversing with the child. Features in both sections are vital for creating and maintaining an optimally rich spoken language-learning environment for a hearing-impaired child. The procedure begins with the caregiver and child being videotaped as they interact during an everyday play or caregiving event. The appropriateness of the parent's role in the videotaped communicative interactions with the child is then studied using the items on the Checklist and their detailed explanations. Having parents be actively involved in this as a self-examination process is probably one of the best ways to inform them about caregiver behaviors which are important for their child's spoken language learning. With varying degrees of guidance, parents are then able to select areas which they want to change as well as to determine how they will go about doing so.

Thus the Checklist can be seen as a tool for making certain that the parent-child relationship and the interactive mechanics are both contributing to an environment optimal for learning spoken language. The expectation is that most of the child's learning will occur in that environment during normal everyday events whose content naturally changes as the child grows and changes.

... NORMAL DEVELOPMENTAL EXPECTATIONS FOR COMMUNICATION, LANGUAGE, AND SPEECH ACHIEVEMENTS ARE CAREFULLY OUTLINED ...

The growth and change observed in normally hearing children's communication, language, and speech development between birth and three years of age are discussed in Chapter 4 of this book. This information can be used for assessing the young hearing-impaired child's general development in those areas as well as for charting progress and predicting or promoting the accomplishments to come. The hearing-impaired child may develop at the same rate as indicated for normally hearing children, or he or she may follow the same sequence at a slower pace, or he or she may not follow the sequence or may not appear to be doing so since the rate is so very slow. All of this is crucially important on-going diagnostic information for professionals and for parents as they plan intervention and make decisions regarding educational placement.

... AND IMPLEMENTATION OF INTERVENTION IS THOROUGHLY ADDRESSED WITH EMPHASES ON THE PARENT, AUDITION, AND SPOKEN LANGUAGE.

The intervention emphasis in this book has been on re-establishing or maintaining a language-learning environment which is normal but enriched in ways which seek to compensate for the effects of the hearing loss. This is appropriate placement for the major emphasis of intervention most of the time, and for most children and parents. However, there are other important parts to intervention as well as other teaching approaches which are useful with some children. In Chapter 6, the notion of there being two intervention agendas is introduced. These agendas are the affect agenda and the content agenda. With regard to the affect agenda, coping with hearing loss in a child is not only a difficult educational issue, but also a difficult emotional one for all involved. Ideally, aural habilitationists have access to social workers, psychologists, and parent groups to assist with families' needs in this area. However, the aural habilitationist needs to be prepared to deal empathically with parental emotions and needs to know when to refer families for additional counselling and support.

The other agenda, the content agenda, includes information the parent needs to absorb about the hearing loss and all of its implications as well as strategies the parent needs to internalize for fostering the child's use of audition and acquisition of intelligible spoken language. Most of those strategies are part of embellished informal teaching. These strategies are used during normal everyday interacting in order to emphasize or highlight particular language, auditory, or speech elements. In addition, with some children it may be useful to use the more deliberate, direct, methodical strategies of semiformal teaching. Unlike most ordinary interacting in this kind of event, the adult has a preplanned goal, play activity, and appropriate materials ready. The child is expected to perform particular tasks, and to say or repeat particular items or phrases. Although some skillful teachers can carry out this kind of activity in ways which keep the child's attention and cooperation, there are two reasons that this semiformal work needs to be viewed with caution. First, the learning may not generalize to more natural situations, and secondly, it violate principles of normal communication and child development. If we want the child to spontaneously, frequently, and creatively engage in meaningful communication as well as to grow up with solid feelings of autonomy, independence, and self-control, then it would be reasonable to create an environment where those elements are fostered. Much of what occurs, even in most regular schools in North America, does not foster those elements. But surely in most cases and most of the time, we can allow our preschool hearing-impaired children to put off encountering that piece of reality by fitting our interventive efforts into the child's normal world of play and being cared for by warm, loving, and nurturing adults. It is the ultimate aim of this book to contribute to that effort.

Glossary

The following are brief explanations of a number of terms found in the text. All of the definitions are appropriate for an aural habilitation context; several items have different meanings in other contexts.

acoustic:	relating to sound
affect:	pertaining to feelings, emotions
alveolar:	a speech sound produced with involvement of the ridge in the mouth just behind the upper teeth, such as /t/ or /d/
amplitude:	the intensity of a sound
bilabial:	a speech sound produced with involvement of the lips, such as /b/ or /m/
caregiver:	any adult who takes care of a child
complementation:	a grammatical term for a particular way of inserting new verbal relationships into sentences (See chapter 4)
conjoining:	a grammatical term for putting together or combining
continuates:	caregiver talk which narrates the obvious
CV syllable:	a consonant-vowel syllable
CVC syllable:	a consonant-vowel-consonant syllable
decibel (dB):	the standard unit for measuring and describing the intensity of a sound
embedded :	a grammatical term for inserting additional information into a sentence

frequency: the measured highness or lowness of a sound, usually measured in Hertz (Hz)

fricatives: speech sounds such as /f/ and /th/ that have turbulent breath flow.

fundamental frequency: the rate at which an individual speaker's vocal chords vibrate in speaking

Hertz: the standard unit for measuring and describing the frequency of a sound

intensity: the measured loudness of a sound, usually described in decibels

intonation: the melody of the voice in speaking

labiodental: a speech sound produced with involvement of the lips and teeth, such as /f/ or /v/

labiolingual: a speech sound produced with involvement of the lips and tongue, such as children's "raspberries"

lexicon: vocabulary; understanding of the meaning(s) of words

localization: being able to determine where a sound is coming from

modality: sensory channel, such as audition, vision, touch

motherese: the way that many mothers (and other caregivers) talk with small children (See Chapter 2)

nasals: speech sounds produced with air emitted from the nose, such as /m/ or /n/

orosensory: tactile sensation in the mouth

peripheral ear: external, middle, and inner ear (not the auditory cortex)

phonation: voicing

phoneme: the smallest meaningful unit of sound in a language

phonemic: pertaining to speech sounds, usually in isolation or in nonsense syllables

phonologic: relating to the use of speech sounds in meaningful language

pitch: the overall highness or lowness of a person's voice or of a speech sound; it can be measured but in this context, it is usually a perceptual estimation

plosives: speech sounds such as /p/, /t/, or /k/ which are produced with a sudden burst of air

pronominal: pertaining to pronouns

prosody: the melody and rhythm of speaking; features of prosody include pitch, intonation, intensity, and duration

resonant voice: a voice strong and rich in overtones

segmentals: consonants and vowels

spectrogram: a graphic illustration of speech sounds displaying intensity, frequency, and duration

suprasegmentals: prosodic speech features such as pitch, intonation, and duration

topicalize: establish topics in conversations

transition time: the time required to move from a consonant to a vowel or from a vowel to a consonant in speaking, usually measured in milliseconds

velar: speech sounds made with the tongue raised near or touching the velum

vibrotactile: sounds which are felt rather than heard

vocalizations: babbling sounds produced by infants

References

American Speech Language Hearing Association (1979). Standards for effective communication programs. *ASHA, 21*, 1002.

Adams, A. K., & Bullock, D. (1986). Apprenticeship in word use: Social convergence processes in learning categorically related nouns. In S. A. Kuczaj & M. D. Barrett (Eds.), *The Development of Word Meaning* (pp. 115–197). New York: Springer-Verlag.

Ames, L. B., & Ilg, F. L. (1976). *Your Two-Year-Old*. New York: Delacorte.

Ames, L. B., Ilg, F. L., & Haber, C. C. (1982a). *Your One-Year-Old: The Fun-loving Fussy 12- to 24-Month Old*. New York: Dell Publishing Co.

Ames, L. B., Ilg, F. L., & Haber, C. C. (1982b). *Your Two-Year-Old: Terrible or Tender*. New York: Dell Publishing Co.

Anderson, B. J. (1979). Parents' strategies for achieving conversational interactions with young hearing-impaired children. In A. Simmons-Martin & D. R. Calvert (Eds.), *Parent-Infant Intervention* (pp. 223–244). New York: Grune and Stratton.

Arco, C. M. B., & McCluskey, K. A. (1981). "A change of pace": An investigation of the salience of maternal temporal style in mother-infant play. *Child Development, 52*, 941–949.

Banigan, R. L., & Mervis, C. B. (1988). Role of adult input in young children's category evolution: II. An experimental study. *Journal of Child Language, 15*, 493–504.

Barnes, S., Gutfreund, M., Satterly, D., & Wells, G. (1983). Characteristics of adult speech which predict children's language development. *Journal of Child Language, 10*, 65–84.

Barrett, M. (1986). Early semantic representations and early word-usage. In S. A. Kuczaj & M. D. Barrett (Eds.), *The Development of Word Meaning* (pp. 39–67). New York: Springer-Verlag.

Bates, E. (1976). *Language and Context: Studies in the Acquisition of Pragmatics.* New York: Academic Press.

Bates, E., Benigni, L., Bretherton, I., Camaioni, L., & Volterra, V. (1979). *The Emergence of Symbols: Cognition and Communication in Infancy.* New York: Academic Press.

Bates, E., Camaioni, L., & Volterra, V. (1975). The acquisition of performatives prior to speech. *Merrill-Palmer Quarterly, 21,* 205–226.

Bates, E., & MacWhinney, B. (1979). A functional approach to the acquisition of grammar. In E. Ochs & B. B. Schieffelin (Eds.), *Developmental Pragmatics* (pp. 167–211). New York: Academic Press.

Bates, E., O'Connell, B., & Shore, C. (1987). Language and communication in infancy. In J. D. Osofsky (Eds.), *Handbook of Infant Development* (pp. 149–203). New York: John Wiley & Sons.

Bates, E., Shore, C., Bretherton, I., & McNew, S. (1983). Names, gestures, and objects: Symbolization in infancy and aphasia. In K. E. Nelson (Eds.), *Children's Language* (*Vol. 4*, pp. 59–123). Hillsdale, NJ: Lawrence Erlbaum.

Bateson, M. C. (1979). The epigenesis of conversational interaction: A personal account of research development. In M. Bullowa (Ed.), *Before Speech: The Beginning of Interpersonal Communication* (pp. 63–77). Cambridge: Cambridge University Press.

Beebe, B., Jaffe, J., Feldstein, S., Mays, K., & Alson, D. (1985). Matching of timing: The application of an adult dialogue model to mother-infant vocal and kinesthetic interactions. In T. Field (Ed.), *Infant Social Perceptions* (pp. 217–241). Norwood, NJ: Ablex.

Beebe, B., & Stern, D. (1977). Engagement-disengagement and early object experience. In N. Freedman & S. Grant (Eds.), *Communicative Structures and Psychic Structures* (pp. 35–55). New York: Plenum Press.

Beebe, H. H., Pearson, H. K., & Koch, M. E. (1984). The Helen Beebe Speech and Hearing Center. In D. Ling (Ed.) *Early Intervention for Hearing-Impaired Children: Oral Options* (pp. 14–63). San Diego, CA: College Hill Press.

Bellinger, D. (1979). Changes in the explicitness of mother's directives as children age. *Journal of Child Language, 6,* 443–455.

Bellinger, D. (1980). Consistency in the pattern of change in mothers' speech: Some discriminant analyses. *Journal of Child Language, 7,* 469–487.

Benedict, H. (1979). Early lexical development: Comprehension and production: *Journal of Child Language, 6,* 183–200.

Bergman, M. (1985). Auditory development and assessment. In S. Harel & N. Anastasiow (Eds.), *The At-risk Infant* (pp. 309–315). Baltimore: Paul H. Brooks.

Best, C. Y., Hoffman, H., & Glanville, B. B. (1982). Development of infant ear asymmetries for speech and music. *Perception and Psychophysics, 31*, 75–85.

Blake, J., & Fink, R. (1987). Sound-meaning correspondances in babbling. *Journal of Child Language, 14*, 229–253.

Blennerhasset, L. (1984). Communication styles of a 13-month-old hearing-impaired child and her parents. *Volta Review, 86*(4), 217–228.

Bloom, K., Russell, A., & Wassenberg, K. (1987). Turn taking affects the quality of infant vocalizations. *Journal of Child Language, 14*, 211–227.

Bloom, L. (1970). *Language Development: Form and Function in Emerging Grammars*. Cambridge, MA: MIT Press.

Bloom, L. (1973). *One Word At a Time: The Use of Single Word Utterances Before Syntax*. The Hague: Mouton.

Bloom, L. (1983). Of continuity, discontinuity, and the magic of language development. In R. M. Golinkoff (Ed.), *The Transition from Prelinguistic to Linguistic Communication* (pp. 79–92). Hillsdale, NJ: Lawrence Erlbaum.

Bloom, L., & Lahey, M. (1978). *Language Development and Language Disorders*. New York: John Wiley & Sons.

Bloom, L., Lahey, M., Hood, L., Lifter, K., & Fiess, K. (1980). Complex sentences: Acquisition of syntactic connectives and the semantic relations they encode. *Journal of Child Language, 7*, 235–261.

Bloom, L., Lightbown, P., Hood, L. (1984). Structure and variation in child language. *Monographs of the Society for Research in Child Development, 40*, (No. 2, Serial No. 160).

Bloom, L., Ripsoli, M., Gartner, B., & Hafitz, J. (1989). Acquisition of complementation. *Journal of Child Language, 16*, 101–120.

Bloom, L., Rocissano, L., & Hood, L. (1976). Adult-child discourse: Developmental interaction between information processing and linguistic knowledge. *Cognitive Psychology, 8*, 521–552.

Bohannan, J. N., & Warren-Leubecker, A. (1985). Theoretical approaches to language acquisition. In J. B. Gleason (Ed.), *The Development of Language* (pp. 173–226). Toronto: Charles J. Merrill.

Boothroyd, A. (1970). *Distribution of Hearing Levels in the Student Population of the Clarke School for the Deaf* (Sensory Aids Research Project No. 3). Northampton, MA: Clarke School for the Deaf.

Boothroyd, A. (1978). Speech perception and sensorineural hearing loss. In M. Ross & T. Giolas (Eds.), *Auditory Management of Hearing-impaired Children* (pp. 117–144). Baltimore: University Park Press.

Bowerman, M. (1978). Systemizing semantic knowledge: changes over time in the child's organization of word meaning. *Child Development, 49*, 977–987.

Bowerman, M. (1982). Reorganizational processes in lexical and syntactic development. In E. Wanner & L. Gleitman (Eds.), *Language Acquisition* (pp. 319–346). Cambridge: Cambridge University Press.

Bowerman, M. (1988). Inducing the latent structure of language. In F. S. Kessel (Ed.), *The Development of Language and Language Researchers: Essays in Honor of Roger Brown* (pp. 23–49). Hillsdale, NJ: Lawrence Erlbaum.

Brazelton, T. B. (1983). *Infants and Mothers* (rev. ed.). New York: Dell Publishing Co.

Brazelton, T. B., Koslowski, B., & Main, M. (1974). The origins of reciprocity. In M. L. Lewis & L. A. Rosenblum (Eds.), *The Effect of the Infant on Its Caregiver* (pp. 49–76). New York: John Wiley & Sons.

Bricker, D., & Casuso, V. (1979). Family involvement: A critical component of early intervention. *Exceptional Children, 46*, 108–116.

Brinich, P. (1980). Childhood deafness and maternal control. *Journal of Communication Disorders, 13*, 75–81.

Brinton, B., & Fujiki, M. (1982). A comparison of request-response sequences in the discourse of normal and language-disorders children. *Journal of Speech and Hearing Disorders, 47*, 57–63.

Broen, P. (1972). The verbal environment of the language-learning child. *ASHA Monograph, 17*.

Bromwich, R. (1981). *Working with Parents and Infants: An Interactional Approach*. Baltimore: University Park Press.

Bronfenbrenner, U. (1974). *Is Early Intervention Effective?* (HEW Publication No. OHD-74-25, Vol. 2). Washington, DC: U.S. Dept. of Health, Education, and Welfare.

Brown, A. (1976). Semantic integration in children's reconstruction of narrative sequences. *Cognitive Psychology, 8*, 247–262.

Brown, R. (1973). *A First Language: The Early Stages*. Cambridge, MA: Harvard University Press.

Brown, R., Cazden, C., & Bellugi-Klima, U. (1969). The child's grammar from I to III. In J. P. Hill (Ed.), *Minnesota Symposia on Child Psychology* (pp. 28–73). Minneapolis, MN: University of Minnesota Press.

Bruner, J. (1975). The ontogenesis of speech acts. *Journal of Child Language, 2*, 1–19.

Bruner, J. (1977). Early social interaction and language acquisition. In H. R. Schaffer (Ed.), *Studies in Mother-Infant Interaction* (pp. 271–289). London: Academic Press.

Bruner, J. (1981). The social context of language acquisition. *Language and Communication, 1*, 155–178.

Bruner, J. (1983). The acquisition of pragmatic commitments. In R. M. Gloinkoff (Ed.), *The Transition from Prelinguistic to Linguistic Communication* (pp. 27–42). Hillsdale, NJ: Lawrence Erlbaum.

Busnel, M. C., & Granier-Deferre, C. (1983). And what of fetal audition? In A. Olivero & M. D. Zappella (Eds.), *The Behavior of Human Infants* (pp. 93–126). New York: Plenum Press.

Carpenter, R. L., Mastergeorge, A. M., & Coggins, T. E. (1983). The acquisition of communicative intentions in infants eight to fifteen months of age. *Language and Speech, 26*, 101–116.

Carter, A. (1979). The disappearance schema: Case study of a second-year communicative behavior. In E. Ochs & B. B. Schieffelin (Eds.), *Developmental Pragmatics* (pp. 131–156). New York: Academic Press.

Chapman, R. (1981). Exploring children's communicative intents. In J. Miller (Ed.), *Assessing Language Production in Children* (pp. 111–136). Baltimore, MD: University Park Press.

Chapman, R., & Miller, J. (1975). Word order in early two and three word utterances: Does production precede comprehension? *Journal of Speech and Hearing Research, 18*, 355–371.

Chomsky, N. (1966). Topics in the theory of generative grammar. In T. Sebeok (Ed.). *Current Trends in Linguistics* (*Vol. 3*, pp. 1–60). The Hague: Mouton.

Clark, E. V., & Carpenter, K. L. (1989). On children's use of *from, by*, and *with* in oblique noun phrases. *Journal of Child Language, 16*, 349–364.

Clark, H., & Clark E. (1979). *Psychology and Language*. New York: Harcourt Brace Jovanich.

Clark, M. (1989). *Language Through Living for Hearing-impaired Children*. London: Hodder & Stroughton.

Clarke-Stewart, K. A. (1973). Interactions between mothers and their young children: Characteristics and consequences. *Monographs of the Society for Research in Child Development, 38* (Nos. 6 and 7, Serial No. 149).

Cole, E. B., & Gregory, H. (Eds), (1986). *Auditory Learning.* Washington, DC: A. G. Bell Association for the Deaf.

Cole, E. B., & St. Clair-Stokes, J. (1984). Caregiver-child interaction behaviors—A videotape analysis procedure. *The Volta Review, 86*(4), 200–216.

Collis, G. (1977). Visual co-orientation and maternal speech. In H. R. Schaffer (Ed.), *Studies in Mother-Infant Interaction* (pp. 355–375). London: Academic Press.

Collis, G., & Schaffer, H. (1975). Synchronization of visual attention in mother-infant pairs. *Journal of Child Psychological Psychiatry, 16,* 315–320.

Constable, C. M. (1983). Creating communication context. In H. Winitz (Ed.), *Treating Language Disorders: For Clinicians by Clinicians* (pp. 97–102). Baltimore: University Park Press.

Conti-Ramsden, G., & Friel-Patti, S. (1987). Situational variability in mother-child conversations. In K. E. Nelson & A. Van Kleek (Eds.), *Children's Language* (*Vol. 6*, pp. 43–63). Hillsdale, NJ: Lawrence Erlbaum.

Conti-Ramsden, G., & Friel-Patti, S. (1983). Mothers' discourse adjustments to language-impaired and non-language-impaired children. *Journal of Speech and Hearing Disorders, 48,* 360–367.

Crago, M.B. (1987). Supervision and self-exploration. In M.B. Crago & M. Pickering (Eds.), *Supervision in Human Communication Disorders: Perspectives on a Process* (pp. 243–278). Boston: Little, Brown & Co.

Crago, M. B. (1988). *Cultural Context in Communicative Interaction of Young Inuit Children.* Unpublished doctoral dissertation, McGill University, Montreal.

Cromer, R. F. (1981). Reconceptualizing language acquisition and cognitive development. In R. L. Schiefelbusch & D. D. Bricker (Eds.), *Early Language: Acquisition and Intervention* (pp. 51–137). Baltimore: University Park Press.

Cross, T. G. (1977). Mother's speech adjustments: The contribution of selected child listener variables. In C. E. Snow & C. A. Ferguson (Eds.), *Talking to Children: Language Input and Acquisition* (pp. 151–188). Cambridge: Cambridge University Press.

Cross, T. G. (1978). Mother's speech and its association with rate of linguistic development in young children. In N. Waterson & C. E. Snow (Eds.), *The Development of Communication: Social and Pragmatic Factors in Language Acquisition* (pp. 199–216). Chichester, NY: John Wiley & Sons.

Cross, T. G. (1984). Habilitating the language-impaired child: Ideas from studies of patent-infant interaction. *Topics in Language Disorders, 4*, 1–14.

Cross, T. G., & Johnson-Morris, J. E. (1980). Linguistic feedback and maternal speech: Comparisons of mothers addressing infants, one year olds, and two year olds. *First Language, 1*, 98–121.

Cross, T. G., Johnson-Morris, J. E., & Nienhuys, T. G. (1980). Linguistic feedback and maternal speech: Comparisons of mothers addressing hearing and hearing-impaired children. *First Language, 1*(3), 163–189.

Cross, T. G., Nienhuys, T. G., & Kirkman, M. (1982). Parent-child interaction with receptively disabled children: Some determinants of maternal speech style. In K. E. Nelson (Ed.), *Children's Language* (*Vol. 5*, pp. 115–152). New York: Gardner Press.

Cross, T. G., Nienhuys, T. G., & Morris, J. E. (1980). Maternal speech styles to deaf and hearing children. *Australian Teacher of the Deaf, 21*, 8—14.

Cryer, D. Helms, T., & Bouland, B. (1988). *Active Learning for Twos*. New York: Addison-Wesley Publishing Co.

Davis, H. (1970). Hearing handicap, standards for hearing, and medicolegal rules. In H. Davis & S. R. Silverman (Eds.), *Hearing and Deafness* (3rd ed.), (pp. 253–279). New York: Holt, Rinehart, & Winston.

DeCasper, A. J., & Fifer, W. P. (1980). Of human bondage: Newborns prefer their mothers' voices. *Sciences, 208*, 1174–1176.

Delack, J. B. (1978). Aspects of infant speech development in the first year of life. *Canadian Journal of Linguistics, 21*, 17–37.

DePaulo, B. N., & Bonvillian, J. D. (1978). The effect on language development of the special characteristics of speech addressed to children. *Journal of Psycholinguistic Research, 7*(3), 189–211.

Doehring, D. G. (1983). Theoretical aspects of auditory perceptual development. In S. E. Gerber & G. T. Mencher (Eds.), *The Development of Auditory Behavior* (pp. 269–286). New York: Grune and Stratton.

Dore, J. (1975). Holophrases, speech acts, and language universals. *Journal of Child Language, 2*, 21–40.

Dore, J. (1978). Conditions for the acquisition of speech acts. In I. Markova (Ed.), *The Social Context of Language* (pp. 87–111). London: John Wiley & Sons.

Dore, J. (1986). The development of conversational competence. In R. L. Schiefelbush (Ed.), *Language Competence: Assessment and Intervention* (pp. 3–60). San Diego CA: College-Hill Press.

Dore, J., Gearhart, M., & Newman, D. (1978). The structure of nursery school conversation. In K. E. Nelson (Ed.), *Children's Language* (*Vol. 1*, pp. 337–395). New York: Gardner Press.

Duchan, J. F. (1986). Language intervention through sense making and fine tuning. In R. L. Schiefelbusch (Ed.), *Language Competence: Assessment and Intervention* (pp. 187–212). San Diego: College-Hill Press.

Edwards, D., & Goodwin, R. (1986). Action words and pragmatic function in early language. In S. A. Kuczaj & M. D. Barrett (Eds.), *The Development of Word Meaning* (pp. 257–273). New York: Springer-Verlag.

Eimas, P. D., Sigueland, E. R., Jusczyk, P., & Vigorito, J. (1971). Speech perception in infants. *Science, 171*, 303–306.

Elbers, L. (1982). Operating principles in repetitive babbling: A cognitive continuity approach. *Cognition, 12*, 45–63.

Ellis, R., & Wells, G. (1980). Enabling factors in adult-child discourse. *First Language, 1*, 46–82.

Emde, R., & Harmon, R. (Eds.), (1984). *Continuities and Discontinuities in Development*. New York: Plenum Press.

Erber, N. P. (19182). *Auditory Training*. Washington, DC: A. G. Bell Association for the Deaf.

Ervin-Tripp, S., & Miller, W. (1977). Early discourse: Some questions about questions. In M. Lewis & L. Rosenblum (Eds.), *Interaction, Conversation, and the Development of Language* (pp. 9–25). New York: John Wiley & Sons.

Fein, G., & Moarin, E. R. (1985). Confusion, substitution, and mastery: Pretend play during the second year of life. In K. E. Nelson (Ed.), *Children's Language* (*Vol. 5*, pp. 61–76). Hillsdale, NJ: Lawrence Erlbaum.

Ferguson, C. (1964). Baby talk in six languages. *American Anthropologist, 66*, 103–114.

Ferguson, C. (1978). Learning to pronounce: The earliest stages of phonological development in the child. In F. D. Minifie & L. L. Lloyd (Eds.), *Communication and Cognitive Abilities - Early Behavioral Assessment* (pp. 273–297). Baltimore, MD: University Park Press.

Fey, M. (1986). *Language Intervention with Young Children*. San Diego, CA: College-Hill Press.

Fitzgerald, M. T., & Fischer, R. M. (1987). A family involvement model for hearing-impaired infants. *Topics in Language Disorders, 7*(3), 1–18.

Folger, J. P., & Chapman, R. S. (1978). A pragmatic analysis of spontaneous imitations. *Journal of Child Language, 5*, 25–38.

Foster, S. (1985). The development of discourse topic skills by infants and young children. *Topics in Language Disorders, 5*, 31–46.

Freedle, R., & Hale, G. (1979). Acquisition of new comprehension schemata for expository prose by transfer of a narrative schema. In R. Freedle (Ed.), *New Directions in Discourse Processing (Vol. 2, pp. 121–135)*. New York: Ablex.

Freedle, R., & Lewis, M. (1977). Prelinguistic conversations. In M. Lewis & L. Rosenblum (Eds.), *Interaction, Conversation, and the Development of Language* (pp. 157–185). New York: John Wiley & Sons.

Fry, D. B. (1966). The development of the phonological system in the normal and the deaf child. In F. Smith & G. A. Miller (Eds.), *The Genesis of Language* (pp. 187–206). Cambridge, MA: M.I.T. Press.

Fry, D. B. (1978). The role and primacy of the auditory channel in speech and language development. In M. Ross & T. G. Giolas (Eds.), *Auditory Management of Hearing-Impaired Children* (pp. 15–43). Baltimore: University Park Press.

Furrow, D., Nelson, K. E., & Benedict, H. (1979). Mothers' speech to children and syntactic development: Some simple relationships. *Journal of Child Language, 6*, 423–442.

Furth, H. (1966). *Thinking Without Language*. New York: Free Press.

Gallagher, T. (1977). Revision behaviors in the speech of normal children developing language. *Journal of Speech and Hearing Research, 70*, 303–318.

Gallagher, T. (1981). Contingent query sentences within adult-child discourse. *Journal of Child Language, 8*, 51–62.

Gallagher, T., & Darnton, B. (1978). Conversational aspects of the speech of language-disordered children: Revision behaviors. *Journal of Speech and Hearing Research, 21*, 118–136.

Gardner, H. (1983). *Frames of Mind*. New York: Basic.

Garland, C., Swanson, J., Stoner, N. W., & Woodruff, G. (Eds.). (1981). *Early Intervention for Children with Special Needs and Their Families*. Monmouth, OR: Westar.

Garnica, O. (1977). Some prosodic and paralinguistic features of speech to young children. In C. E. Snow & C. A. Ferguson (Eds.), *Talking to Children: Language Input and Acquisition* (pp. 63–88). Cambridge: Cambridge University Press.

Garvey, C. (1977). The contingent query: A dependent act in conversation. In M. L. Lewis & L. A. Rosenblum (Eds.), *Interaction, Conversation, and the Development of Language* (pp. 63–93). New York: John Wiley & Sons.

Geers, A., & Moog, J. (1989). Factors predicting the development of literacy in profoundly hearing-impaired adolescents. *Volta Review, 91*(2), 69–86.

Gersh, M. J. (1966). *How to Raise Children at Home in Your Spare Time.* New York: Stein & Day.

Ginsburg, G. P., & Kilbourne, B. K. (1988). Emergence of vocal alternation in mother-infant interaction. *Journal of Child Language, 15,* 221–235.

Gleason, J., Perlmann, P., & Grief, E. (1984). What's the magic word: Learning language through politeness routines. *Discourse Processes, 7,* 493–502.

Gleitman, L. R., Newport. E. I., & Gleitman, H. (1984). The current status of the motherese hypothesis. *Journal of Child Language, 11,* 43–79.

Glover, M. E., Preminger, J. L., & Sanford, A. R. (1978). *The Early Learning Accomplishment Profile for Developmentally Young Children: Birth to 36 Months.* Winston-Salem, NC: Kaplan Press.

Goldberg, S. (1977). Social competence in infancy: A model of parent-infant interaction. *Merrill-Palmer Quarterly, 23,* 163–178.

Golinkoff, R. M. (Ed.). (1983). *The Transition from Prelinguistic to Linguistic Communication.* Hillsdale, NJ: Lawrence Erlbaum.

Gopnik, A. (1988). Three types of early words: The emergence of social words, names, and cognitive relational words in the one-word stage and their relation to cognitive development. *First Language, 8,* 49–70.

Gorga, M. P., Kaminski, J. R., Beauchaine, K. L., Jesteadt, W., & Neeley, S. T. (1989). Auditory responses from children three months to three years of age: Normal patterns of response II. *Journal of Speech and Hearing Research, 32*(2), 281–297.

Greenfield, P., Reilly, J., Leaper, C., & Baker, N. (1985). The structural and functional status of single-word utterances and their relationship to early multi-word speech. In M. Barrett (Ed.), *Children's Single-Word Speech* (pp. 233–267). New York: John Wiley & Sons.

Greenfield, P., & Smith, J. (1976). *The Structure of Communication in Early Language Development.* New York: Academic Press.

Greenstein, J. M., Greenstein, B. B., McConville, K., & Stellini, L. (1975). *Mother-Infant Communication and Language Acquisition in Deaf Infants.* New York: Lexington School for the Deaf.

Gregory, S., Mogford, K., & Bishop, J. (1979). Mother's speech to young hearing-impaired children. *Journal of Child Language, 8,* 35–49.

Grice, H. (1975). Logic and conversation. In M. Cole & J. Morgan (Eds.), *Syntax and Semantics* (*Vol. 3,* pp. 41–58). New York: Academic Press.

Griffiths, C. (1955). *The Utilization of Individual Hearing Aids on Young Deaf Children*. Unpublished doctoral dissertation, University of Southern California, Los Angeles.

Griffiths, C. (1964). The auditory approach for preschool deaf children. *Volta Review, 66*(7), 387–397.

Griffiths, C., & Ebbin, J. (1978). *Effectiveness of Early Detection and Auditory Stimulation on the Speech and Language of Hearing-Impaired Children* (Contract No. HSM 110-69-431). Washington, DC: Health Services Administration.

Halliday, M. A. K. (1975). *Learning How to Mean: Exploration in the Development of Language*. London: Arnold.

Hamburger, H., & Crain, S. (1982) Relative acquisition. In S. A. Kuczaj (Ed.), *Language Development: Vol. 1. Syntax and Semantics* (pp. 245–274). Hillsdale, NJ: Lawrence Erlbaum.

Harding, C. G. (1983). Setting the stage for language acquisition: Communication development in the first year. In R. M. Golinkoff (Ed.), *The Transition From Prelinguistic to Linguistic Communication* (pp. 93–113). Hillsdale, NJ: Lawrence Erlbaum.

Harste, J. C., Woodward, V. A., & Burke C. (1984). *Language Stories and Literacy Lessons*. Portsmouth, NH: Heinemann Educational Press.

Hasenstab, M. S., & Horner, J. (1982). *Comprehensive Intervention with Hearing-impaired Infants and Preschool Children*. Rockville, MD: Aspen Systems Corporation.

Hecox, K. (1975). Electrophysiological correlates of human auditory development. In L. B. Cohen & P. Salapatek (Eds.), *Infant Perception: From Sensation to Cognition* (Vol. 2, pp. 151–191). New York: Academic Press.

Hirsch, I. J. (1970). Auditory training. In H. Davis & S. Silverman (Eds.), *Hearing and Deafness* (pp. 346–359). New York: Holt, Rinehart, & Winston.

Hoff-Ginsberg, E., & Shatz, M. (1982). Linguistic input and the child's acquisition of language. *Psychological Bulletin, 92*, 3–26.

Horton, K. (1974). Infant intervention and language learning. In R. L. Schiefelbusch & L. L. Lloyd (Eds.), *Language Perspectives: Acquisition, Retardation, and Intervention* (pp. 469–491). Baltimore: University Park Press.

Howe, C. J. (1981). *Acquiring Language in Conversational Context*. New York: Academic Press.

Hymes, D. (1972). On communicative competence. In J. B. Pride & J. Holmes (Eds.), *Sociolinguistics* (pp. 269–293). New York: Penguin Books.

Ingram, D. (1986). Phonological development production. In P. Fletcher & M. Gorman (Eds.), *Language Acquisition: Studies in First Language* (2nd ed., pp. 223–239). Cambridge, UK: C.U.P.

Jaffee, J. D., Stern, D, & Peery, J. (1973). 'Conversational' coupling of gaze behavior in prelinguistic human development. *Journal of Psycholingusitic Research, 2*, 321–330.

Jeremy, R. J. (1978). Use of coordinate sentences with the conjunction "and" for describing temporal and locative relations between events. *Journal of Psycholinguistic Research, 7*, 135–150.

Kaye, K. (1980). Why we don't talk "baby talk" to babies. *Journal of Child Language, 7*, 489–507.

Kaye, K. (1982). *The Mental and Social Life of Babies: How Parents Create Persons.* Chicago, IL: University of Chicago Press.

Kaye, K., & Charney, R. (1980). How mothers maintain "dialogue" with two-year-olds. In D. Olson (Ed.), *The Social Foundations of Language and Thought* (pp. 211–230). New York: Norton.

Kaye, K., & Charney, R. (1981). Conversation asymmetry between mothers and children. *Journal of Child Language, 8*, 35–50.

Kaye, K., & Wells, A. (1980). Mothers' jiggling and the burst-pause pattern in neonatal sucking. *Infant Behavior and Development, 3*, 29–46.

Keller-Cohen, D. (1978). Context in child language. *Annual Review of Anthropology, 7*, 453–482.

Kent, R. D., & Bauer, H. R. (1985). Vocalization of one-year-olds. *Journal of Child Language, 13*, 491–526.

Klevans, D. R. (1988). Counseling strategies for communication disorders. In R. F. Curlee (Ed.), *Counseling in Speech, Language, Hearing, Seminars in Speech and Language, 9*(3), 185–208.

Kretschmer, R. R., & Kretschmer, L. W. (1978). *Language Development and Intervention with the Hearing Impaired.* Baltimore: University Park Press.

Kubler-Ross, E. (1969). *On Death and Dying.* New York: MacMillan Publishing Co.

Kuczaj, S. A. (1986). Thoughts on the intentional basis of early object word extension: Evidence from comprehension and production. In S. A. Kuczaj & M. D. Barrett (Eds.), *The Development of Word Meaning* (pp. 99–120). New York: Springer-Verlag.

Kuhl, P. K. (1979). The perception of speech in early infancy. In N. J. Lass (Ed.), *Speech and Language: Advances in Basic Research and Practice* (pp. 1–47). New York: Academic Press.

Kuhl, P. K. (1981). Auditory category formation and developmental speech perception. In R. E. Stark (Ed.), *Language Behavior in Infancy and Early Childhood* (pp. 165–181). North Holland: Elsevier.

Kuhl, P. K. (1983). The perception of speech in early infancy: Four phenomena. In S. E. Gerber & G. T. Mencher (Eds.), *The Development of Auditory Behavior* (pp. 187–218). New York: Grune and Stratton.

Kuhl, P. K. (1987). Perception of speech and sound in early infancy. In P. Salapatek & L. Cohen (Eds.), *Handbook of Infant Perceptions: From Perception to Cognition* (*Vol. 2*, pp. 275–382). New York: Academic Press.

Lahey, M. (1988). *Language Disorders and Language Development*. New York: MacMillan.

Lasky, E. Z. & Klopp, K. (1982). Parent-child interactions in normal and language-disordered children. *Journal of Speech and Hearing Disorders, 47,* 7–18.

Leach, P. (1976). *Babyhood.* New York: Alfred A. Knopf.

Lieberman, P. (1980). On the development of vowel production in young children. In G. Yeni-Komshian, J. Kavanaugh, & C. A. Ferguson (Eds.), *Child Phonology: Vol. 1 Production* (pp. 113–142). New York: Academic Press.

Lieven, E. V. M. (1978a). Conversation between mothers and young children: Individual differences and their possible implications for the study of language learning. In N. Waterson & C. E. Snow (Eds.), *The Development of Communication: Social and Pragmatic Factors in Language Acquisition* (pp. 173–189). London: Wiley.

Lieven, E. V. M. (1978b). Turn-taking and pragmatics: Two issues in early child language. In R. Campbell & P. Smith (Eds.), *Advances in the Psychology of Language* (pp. 215–236). New York: Plenum Press.

Lieven, E. V. M. (1980) *Language Development in Young Children.* Unpublished doctoral dissertation, Cambridge University.

Lieven, E. V. M. (1984). Interactional styles and children's language learning. *Topics in Language Disorders, 4*(4), 15–23.

Limber, J. (1973). The genesis of complex sentences. In T. Moore (Ed.), *Cognitive Development and the Acquisition of Language* (pp. 169–185). New York: Academic Press.

Lindfors, J. W. (1980). *Children's Language and Learning* (2nd ed.). Englewood Cliffs, NJ: Prentice-Hall.

Ling, D. (1964). An auditory approach to the education of deaf children. *Audecibel, 13*, 96–101.

Ling, D. (1976). *Speech and the Hearing-Impaired Child: Theory and Practice.* Washington, DC: A. G. Bell Association for the Deaf.

Ling, D. (1978). Auditory coding and reading: An analysis of auditory training procedures for hearing-impaired children. In M. Ross & T. G. Giolas (Eds.), *Auditory Management of Hearing-impaired Children* (pp. 181–218). Baltimore: University Park Press.

Ling, D. (1981). Keep your hearing-impaired child within earshot. *Newsounds, 6*, 5–6.

Ling, D. (1986a). Devices and procedures for auditory learning. In E. B. Cole, & H. Gregory (Eds.), *Auditory Learning* (pp. 19–28). Washington, DC: A. G. Bell Association for the Deaf.

Ling, D. (1986b). *Early Intervention for Hearing-impaired Children: Oral Options.* San Diego, CA: College Hill Press.

Ling, D. (1989). *Foundations of Spoken Language for Hearing-impaired Children.* Washington, DC: A. G. Bell Association for the Deaf.

Ling, D., Leckie, D., Pollack, D., Simser, J., & Smith, A. (1981). Syllable reception by profoundly hearing-impaired children trained from infancy in auditory-oral programs. *Volta Review, 83*, 451–465.

Ling, D., & Ling, N. (1978). *Aural Habilitation: The Foundations of Verbal Learning in Hearing-Impaired Children.* Washington, DC: A. G. Bell Association for the Deaf.

Ling, D., & Milne, M. (1981). The development of speech in hearing-impaired children. In F. Bess, B. A. Freeman, & J. S. Sinclair (Eds.), *Amplification in Education* (pp. 98–108). Washington, DC: A. G. Bell Association for the Deaf.

Locke, J. L. (1983). *Phonological Acquisition and Changes.* New York: Academic Press.

Locke, J. L. (1986). Speech perception and the emergent lexicon: An ethological approach. In P. Fletcher & M. Gorman (Eds.), *Language Acquisition: Studies in First Language* (2nd ed., pp. 240–268). Cambridge UK: C.U.P.

Los Angeles County Public Schools. (1976). *Forework's Auditory Skills Curriculum* (A component of the Auditory Skills Instructional Planning System [ASIPS]). P.O. Box 9747, North Hollywood, CA 91606.

Lowell, E. L., & Stoner, M. (1960). *Play It By Ear.* Los Angeles, CA: John Tracy Clinic.

Lowy, L. (1983). Social work supervision: From models toward theory. *Journal of Education for Social Work, 19*, 55–62.

Lucas, E. (1980). *Semantic and Pragmatic Language Disorders: Assessment and Remediation*. Rockville, MD: Aspen System Corp.

Lucariello, J. (1987). Concept formation and its relation to word learning and use in the second year. *Journal of Child Language, 14*, 309–332.

Luterman, D. (1976). A comparison of language skills of hearing-impaired children trained in a visual/oral methods and an auditory/oral method. *American Annals of the Deaf, 121*, 389–393.

Luterman, D. (1979). *Counseling Parents of Hearing-Impaired Children*. Boston, MA: Little, Brown, & Co.

Luterman, D. (1984). *Counseling the Communicatively Disordered and Their Families*. Boston, MA: Little, Brown, & Co.

Luterman, D. (1987). *Deafness in the Family*. Boston, MA: Little, Brown, Co.

MacNamara, J. (1972). Cognitive basis of language learning in infants. *Psychological Review, 77*, 282–293.

Markides, A. (1986). The use of residual hearing in the education of hearing-impaired children: A historical perspective. In E. B. Cole, & H. Gregory (Eds.), *Auditory Learning* (pp. 57–66). Washington, DC: A. G. Bell Association for the Deaf.

Martin, J. A. (1981). A longitudinal study of the consequence of early mother-infant interaction: A micro-analytic approach. *Monographs of the Society for Research in Child Development, 46* (No. 3, Serial No. 190).

Martlew, M. (1980). Mothers' control strategies in dyadic mother-child conversations. *Journal of Psycholinguistic Research, 9*, 327–347.

Matey, C., & Kretschmer, R. (1985). A comparison of mother speech to Down's syndrome, hearing-impaired, normal-hearing children. *Volta Review, 87*(4), 205–213.

McDade, H. L., & Varnedoe, D. R. (1987). Training parents to be language facilitators. *Topics in Language Disorders, 7*(3), 19–30.

McDonald, L. & Pien, D. (1982). Mother conversational behaviors as a function of interactional intent. *Journal of Child Language, 9*, 337–358.

McNiell, D. (1966). Developmental psycholinguistics. In F. Smith & G. A. Miller (Eds.), *The Genesis of Language: A Psycholinguistic Approach* (pp. 15–84). Cambridge, MA: M.I.T. Press.

McWilliams, B. J. (1976). Various aspects of parent counseling. In E. J. Webster (Ed.), *Professional Approaches with Parents of Handicapped Children* (pp. 27–64). Springfield, IL: Charles C Thomas.

Mehler, J., Bertoncini, J., Barriere, M., & Jassik-Geschenfeld, D. (1978). Infant recognition of mother's voice. *Perception, 7*, 491–497.

Mervis, C. B., & Crisalfi, M. A. (1982). Order of acquisition of subordinate-, basic-, and superordinate-level categories. *Child Development, 53*, 258–266.

Mervis, C. B., & Mervis, C. A. (1982). Leopards are kitty-cats: Object labelling by mothers for their thirteen-month-olds. *Child Development, 53*, 267–272.

Mervis, C. B., & Mervis, C. A. (1988). Role of adult input in young children's category evolution: I. An observational study. *Journal of Child Language, 15*, 257–272.

Miller, C. L. (1988). Parents' perceptions and attributions of infant vocal behavior and development. *First Language, 8*, 125–141.

Miller, P. J., & Sperry, L. L. (1988). Early talk about the past: The origins of conversational stories of personal experience. *Journal of Child Language, 25*, 293–315.

Milne, A. A. (1926). *Winnie-the-Pooh*. New York: Dutton.

Mishler, E. G. (1979). Meaning in context: Is there any other kind? *Harvard Educational Review, 49*, 1–19.

Missouri Dept. of Elementary & Secondary Education. (1982). *How Does Your Child Grow and Learn: A Guide for Parents of Young Children*. P.O. Box 480, Jefferson City, MO 65102.

Moses, K. (1979). Parenting a hearing-impaired child. *Volta Review, 81*, 73–80.

Moses, K. (1985). Infant deafness and parental grief: Psychosocial early intervention. In F. Powell, T. Finitzo-Hieber, S. Friel-Patti, & D. Henderson (Eds.), *Education of the Hearing-Impaired Child* (pp. 86–102). San Diego, CA: College-Hill Press.

Moses, K., & Van Hecke-Wulatin, M. (1981). The socio-emotional impact of infant deafness: A counselling model. In G. T. Mencher & S. E. Gerber (Eds.), *Early Management of Hearing Loss* (pp. 243–278). New York: Grune and Stratton.

Murphy, A. T. (1976). Parent counseling and exceptionality: From creative insecurity toward increasing humanness. In E. J. Webster (Ed.), *Professional Approaches with Parents of Handicapped Children* (pp. 3–26). Springfield, IL: Charles C Thomas.

Myklebust, H. (1960). *The Psychology of Deafness*. New York: Grune and Stratton.

Nelson, K. E. (1973). Structure and strategy in learning to talk. *Monographs of the Society for Research in Child Development, 38* (Serial No. 149).

Nelson, K. E. (1976). Facilitating children's syntax. *Developmental Psychology, 13*, 101–107.

Nelson, K. E. (1981). Individual differences in language development: Implications for development and language. *Developmental Psychology, 17*, 170–187.

Nelson, K. E., Bonvillian, J., Denninger, M., Kaplan, B., & Baker, N. (1984). Maternal input adjustments and nonadjustments as related to children's linguistic advances and to language acquisition theories. In A. Pellegrini & T. Yawkey (Eds.), *The Development of Oral and Written Language in Social Contexts* (pp. 31–56). Norwood, NJ: Ablex.

Nelson, K. E., Carskaddon, G., & Bonvillian, J. D. (1973). Syntax acquisition: Impact of environmental assistance in adult verbal interaction with the child. *Child Development, 44*, 497–504.

Newport, E. (1977). Motherese: The speech of mothers to young children. In N. Castellan, D. Pisoni, & G. Potts (Eds.), *Cognitive Theory (Vol. 2*, pp. 69–84). Hillsdale, NJ: Lawrence Erlbaum.

Newport, E. L., Gleitman, H., & Gleitman, L. R. (1977). Mother, I'd rather do it myself: Some effects and non-effects of maternal speech style. In C. E. Snow & C. A. Ferguson (Eds.), *Talking to Children: Language Input and Acquisition* (pp. 109–149). Cambridge: Cambridge University Press.

Newson, J. (1977). The growth of shared understandings between infant and caregiver. In M. Bullowa (Ed.), *Before Speech: The Beginning of Interpersonal Communication* (pp. 207–222). Cambridge: Cambridge University Press.

Nienhuys, T. G., Cross, T. G., & Horsborough, K. M. (1984). Child variables influencing maternal speech style: Deaf and hearing children. *Journal of Communication Disorders, 17*, 189–207.

Northcott, W. H. (Ed.). (1977). *Curriculum Guide for Hearing-Impaired Children - Birth to Three Years - and Their Parents*. Washington, DC: A. G. Bell Association for the Deaf.

Northcott, W. H. (Ed.). (1978) *I heard that! A Development Sequence of Listening Activities for the Young Child*. Washington, DC: A. G. Bell Association for the Deaf.

Northern, J. L., & Downs, M. P. (1978). *Hearing in Children* (2nd ed.). Baltimore: Williams & Wilkins.

Ochs, E., & Schieffelin, B. B. (Eds.) (1979). *Development Pragmatics*. New York: Academic Press.

Oller, D. K. (1977). Infant vocalization and the development of speech. *Allied Health and Behavioral Sciences, 1*(4), 523–549.

Oller, D. K. (1980). The emergence of speech sounds in infancy. In G. Yeni-Komshian, J. Kavanaugh, & C. A. Ferguson (Eds.), *Child Phonology: Vol. 1 Production* (pp. 93–112). New York: Academic Press.

Oller, D. K. (1983). Infant babbling as a manifestation of the capacity for speech. In S. E. Gerber & G. T. Mencher (Eds.), *The Development of Auditory Behavior* (pp. 221–235). New York: Grune and Stratton.

Olsen-Fulero, L. (1982). Style and stability in mother conversational behavior: A study of individual differences. *Journal of Child Language, 9*, 543–564.

Olsen-Fulero, L., & Conforti, J. (1983). Child responsiveness to mother questions of varying type and presentation. *Journal of Child Language, 10*, 495–520.

Pea, R. D. (1980). The development of negation in early child language. In D. R. Olson (Ed.), *The Social Foundations of Language and Thought* (pp. 221–245). New York: Norton.

Peece, A. (1987). The range of narrative forms conversationally produced by young children. *Journal of Child Language, 14*, 353–373.

Peters, A. (1983). *The Units of Language Acquisition*. Cambridge: Cambridge University Press.

Peters, A. M., & Boggs, S. T. (1986). Interactional routines as cultural references upon language acquisition. In B. B. Schieffelin & B. Ochs (Eds.), *Language Socialization Across Cultures*. Cambridge: Cambridge University Press.

Peterson, C. F., Donner, F., & Flavell, J. (1972). Developmental changes in children's responses to three indications of communication failure. *Child Development, 43*, 1463–1468.

Peterson, G. A., & Sherrod, K. B. (1982). Relationship of maternal language to language development and language delay of children. *American Journal of Mental Deficiency, 86*, 391–398.

Pflaster, G. (1980). A factor analysis of variables relating to academic performance of hearing-impaired children in regular classes. *Volta Review, 82*(2), 71–84.

Pflaster, G. (1981). A second analysis of factors related to the academic performance of hearing-impaired children in the mainstream. *Volta Review, 83*(2), 71–80.

Phillips, J. (1973). Syntax and vocabulary of mother's speech to young children: Age and sex comparisons. *Child Development, 44*, 182–185.

Pickering, M. (1987). Interpersonal communication and the supervisory process: A search for Ariadne's thread. In M. Crago & M. Pickering (Eds.), *Supervision in Human Communication Disorders: Perspectives on a Process* (pp. 203–225). Boston: Little, Brown, & Co.

Pinker, S. (1984). *Language Learnability and Language Development*. Cambridge, MA: Harvard University Press.

Pollack, D. (1970). *Educational Audiology for the Limited-Hearing Infant* (1st ed.). Springfield, IL: Charles C Thomas.

Pollack, D. (1985). *Educational Audiology for the Limited-Hearing Infant and Preschooler* (2nd ed.). Springfield, IL: Charles C Thomas.

Pollack, D., & Ernst, M. (1974). An acoupedic program. In C. Griffiths (Ed.), *Proceedings of the International Conference on Auditory Techniques* (pp. 139–164). Springfield, IL: Charles C Thomas.

Prather, E. M., Hedrick, D. L., & Kern, C. A. (1975). Articulation development in children aged two to four years. *Journal of Speech and Hearing Disorders, 40*, 179–191.

Proctor, A. (1989). Stages of noncry vocal development in infancy: A protocol for assessment. *Topics in Language Disorders, 10*, 26–42.

Prutting, C. A. (1982). Pragmatics as social competence. *Journal of Speech and Hearing Disorders, 47*, 123–134.

Retherford, K. S., Schwartz, B. C., & Chapman, R. S. (1981). Semantic roles and residual grammatical categories in mother and child speech: Who tunes in to whom? *Journal of Child Language, 8*, 583–608.

Rice, M. L. (1986). Mismatched premises of the communicative competence model and language intervention. In R. L. Schiefelbusch (Ed.), *Language Competence: Assessment and Intervention* (pp. 261–280). San Diego, CA: College-Hill Press.

Riesen, A. H. (1974). Studies of early sensory deprivation in animals. In C. Griffiths (Ed.), *Proceedings of the International Conference on Auditory Techniques* (pp. 33–38). Springfield, IL: Charles C Thomas.

Rocissano, L., & Yatchmink, Y. (1983). Language skill and interactive patterns in prematurely born toddlers. *Child Development, 54*, 1229–1241.

Roe, K. V., McClure, A., & Roe, A., (1982). Vocal interaction at 3 months and cognitive skills at 12 years. *Developmental Psychology, 18*, 15–16.

Rogers, C. (1951). *Client-Centered Therapy*. Boston, MA: Houghton Mifflin.

Rosen, S., Walliker, J., Brimacombe, J. A., & Edgerton, B. J. (1989). Prosodic and segmental aspects of speech perception with the House/3 M single-channel implant. *Journal of Speech and Hearing Research, 32*(1), 93–111.

Roth, F. P., & Spekman, N. J. (1984). Assessing the pragmtic abilities of children: Part I: Organization framework and assessment parameters. *Journal of Speech and Hearing Disorders, 49*, 2–11.

Roth, P. L. (1987). Temporal characteristics of maternal verbal styles. In K. E. Nelson & A. Van Kleek (Eds.), *Children's Language (Vol.6*, pp. 137–158). Hillsdale, NJ: Lawrence Erlbaum.

Rutter, D., & Durkin, K. (1987). Turn-taking in mother-infant interaction: An examination of vocalizations and gaze. *Developmental Psychology, 23*, 54–61.

Sachs, J. (1977). The adaptive significance of linguistic input to prelinguistic infants. In C. E. Snow & C. A. Ferguson (Eds.), *Talking to Children: Language Input and Acquisition* (pp. 51–61). Cambridge: Cambridge University Press.

Sachs, J. (1979). Topic selection in parent-child discourse. *Discourse Processes, 2*, 145–153.

Sachs, J. (1983). Talking about the there and then: The emergence of displaced reference in parent-child discourse. In K. E. Nelson (Ed.), *Children's Language (Vol. 4*, pp. 1–28). Hillsdale, NJ: Lawrence Erlbaum.

Sacks, H., Schegloff, E., & Jefferson, G. (1974). A simplest systematics for the organization of turn-taking for conversation. *Language, 50*, 696–735.

Sanders, D. A. (1982). *Aural Rehabilitation* (2nd ed.). Englewood Cliffs, NJ: Prentice-Hall, Inc.

Scaife, M., & Bruner, J. (1975). The capacity for joint visual attention in the infant. *Nature, 253*, 265–268.

Schaffer, H. R., Collis, G., & Parsons, G. (1977). Vocal interchange and visual regard in verbal and pre-verbal children. In H. R. Schaffer (Ed.), *Studies in Mother-Infant Interaction* (pp. 291–324). London: Academic Press.

Scherer, N., & Olswang, L. (1984). Role of mothers' expansions in stimulating children's language production. *Journal of Speech and Hearing Research, 27*, 387–396.

Schieffelin, B. B., & Eisenberg, A. R. (1984). Culture variation in children's conversation. In R. L. Schiefelbush & J. P. Pickar (Eds.), *The Acquisition of Communicative Competence* (pp. 377–420). Baltimore: University Park Press.

Schlesinger, H. S., & Meadow, K. P. (1972). *Sound and Sign*. Berkeley, CA: University of California Press.

Schneider, B. A., Trehub, S. E., & Bull, D. (1979). The development of basic auditory processes in infants. *Canadian Journal of Psychology, 33*, 306–319.

Schneider, B. A., Trehub, S. E., & Bull, D. (1980). High-frequency sensitivity in infants. *Science, 207*, 1003–1004.

Schodorf, J. K. (1982). A comparative analysis of parent-child interactions of language-delayed and linguistically normal children. *Dissertation Abstracts International, 42*(5), 1838-B.

Schuyler, V., & Rushmer, N. (1987). *Parent-Infant Habilitation: A Comprehensive Approach to Working with Hearing-Impaired Infants and Toddlers and Their Families.* Portland, OR: Infant: Hearing Resource.

Schwartz, S., & Miller, J. E. H. (1988). *The Language of Toys: Teaching Communication Skills to Special Needs Children.* Kensington, MD: Woodbine House.

Seitz, S., & Stewart, C. (1975). Imitation and expansion: Some developmental aspects of mother-child conversation. *Developmental Psychology, 11*, 763–768.

Shatz, M. (1987). Bootstrapping operations in child language. In K. E. Nelson & A. Van Kleek (Eds.), *Children's Language* (Vol. 6, pp. 1–22). Hillsdale, NJ: Lawrence Erlbaum.

Sherrer, K. R. (1974). Acoustic concomitants of emotional dimensions: Judging affect from synthesized tone sequences. In J. Weitz (Ed.), *Nonverbal Communication* (pp. 145–180). Oxford: Oxford University Press.

Shontz, F. (1965). Reactions to crisis. *Volta Review, 67*, 364–370.

Sitnick, V., Rushmer, N., & Arpan, R. (1977). *Parent-Infant Communication: A Program of Clinical and Home Training for Parents and Hearing-impaired infants.* Beaverton, OR: Dormac.

Skinner, B. F. (1957). *Verbal Behavior.* New York: Appleton-Century-Crofts.

Skinner, B. F. (1964). New methods and new dimensions in teaching. *New Scientist, 22*(392), 483–484.

Slobin, D. I. (1973). Cognitive prerequisites for the development of grammar. In C. A. Ferguson & D. I. Slobin (Eds.), *Studies of Child Language Development* (pp. 175–208). New York: Holt, Rinehart, and Winston.

Smith, B. J., & Strain, P. S. (1988). Does early intervention help? *ERIC Digest, 455*, 1–2.

Snow, C. E. (1972). Mother's speech to children learning language. *Child Development, 43*, 549–565.

Snow, C. E. (1977). The development of conversation between mothers and babies. *Journal of Child Language, 4*, 1–22.

Snow, C. E. (1978). Why routines are different: Toward a multiple-factors model of the relation between input and language acquisition. In K. E. Nelson & A. van Kleeck (Eds.), *Children's Language (Vol. 6*, pp. 65–97). Hillsdale, NJ: Lawrence Erlbaum.

Snow, C. E. (1984a). Parent-child interaction and the development of communicative ability. In R. L. Schiefelbusch & J. P. Pickar (Eds.), *The Acquisition of Communicative Competence* (pp. 69–107). Baltimore: University Park Press.

Snow, C. E. (1984b). Foreword. *Topics in Language Disorders, 4*(4), v.

Snow, C. E., deBlauw, S., & van Roosmalen, G. (1979). Talking and playing with babies: The role of ideologies of childrearing. In M. Bullowa (Ed.), *Before Speech: The Beginning of Interpersonal Communication* (pp. 269–288). Cambridge: Cambridge University Press.

Snow, C. E., & Ferguson, C. A. (Eds.) (1977). *Talking To Children: Language Input and Acquisition.* Cambridge: Cambridge University Press.

Snow, C. E., & Gilbreath, B. J. (1983). Explaining transitions. In R. M. Golinkoff (Ed.), *The Transition From Prelinguistic to Linguistic Communication* (pp. 281–296). Hillsdale, NJ: Lawrence Erlbaum.

Snow, C. E., & Goldfield, B. A. (1983). Turn the page please: Situation-specific language learning. *Journal of Child Language, 10,* 551–570.

Snow, C. E., Midkiff-Borunda, S., Small, A., & Proctor, A. (1984) Therapy as social interaction: Analyzing the context of language remediation. *Topics in Language Disorders, 4,* 72–85.

Snow, C. E., Perlman, R., & Nathan, D. (1987). Why routines are different: Toward a multiple-factors model of the relation between input and language acquisition. In K. E. Nelson & A. Van Kleek (Eds.), *Children's Language (Vol. 6,* pp. 65–97). Hillsdale, NJ: Lawrence Erlbaum.

Spock, B., & Rothenberg, M. B. (1985). *Dr. Spock's Baby and Child Care* (rev. ed.). New York: Simon & Schuster.

Staats, A. (1971). Linguistic-mentalistic theory versus an explanatory S-R learning theory of language development. In D. Slobin (Ed.), *The Ontogenesis of Grammar* (pp. 103–150). New York Academic Press.

Stark, R. E. (1978). Infant speech production and communication skills. *Allied Health and Behavioral Sciences, 1*(2), 131–151.

Stark, R. E. (1980). Stages of speech development in the first year of life. In G. Yeni-Komshian, J. Kavanaugh, & C. A. Ferguson (Eds.), *Child Phonology: Vol. 1. Production* (pp. 73–92). New York: Academic Press.

Stella-Prorok, E. M. (1983). Mother-child language in the natural environment. In K. E. Nelson (Ed.), *Children's Language* (*Vol. 4*, pp. 187–230). New York: Gardner Press.

Stern, D. N. (1974). Mother and infant at play: The dyadic interaction involving facial, vocal, and gaze behaviors. In M. L. Lewis & L. A. Rosenblum (Eds.), *The Effects of the Infant on Its Caregiver* (pp. 187–213). New York: John Wiley & Sons.

Stern, D. N., Spieker, S., Barnett, R. K., & MacKain, K. (1983). The prosody of maternal speech: Infant age and context-related changes. *Journal of Child Language, 10*, 1–16.

Stone, P. (1983). Auditory learning in a school setting: Procedures and results. *Volta Review, 85*(1), 7–13.

Streng, A. H., Kretschmer, R. R., & Kretschmer, L. K. (1978). *Language, Learning and Deafness*. New York: Grune and Stratton.

Sugarman, S. (1983). Empirical versus logical issues in the transition from prelinguistic to linguistic communication. In R. M. Golinkoff (Ed.), *The Transition from Prelinguistic to Linguistic Communication* (pp. 133–145). Hillsdale, NJ: Lawrence Erlbaum.

Sugarman, S. (1984). The development of communication: Its contribution and limits in promoting the development of language. In R. L. Schifelbusch & J. P. Pickar (Eds.), *The Acquisition of Communicative Competence* (pp. 23–67). Baltimore: University Park Press.

Sweitzer, R. S. (1977). Audiologic evaluation of the infant and young child. In B. F. Jaffe (Ed.), *Hearing Loss in Children* (pp. 101–131). Baltimore: University Park Press.

Tager-Flushberg, H., de Villiers, J. G., & Hakuta, K. (1982). The development of sentence coordination. In S. A. Kuczaj (Ed.), *Language Development: Vol. 1. Syntax and Semantics* (pp. 201–243). Hillsdale, NJ: Lawrence Erlbaum.

Teale, W. H., & Sulzby, E. (Eds.). (1986). *Emergent Literacy: Writing and Reading*. Norwood, NJ: Ablex.

Tees, R. C. (1967). Effects of early auditory restrictions in the rat on adult pattern discrimination. *Journal of Comparative and Physiological Psychology, 63*, 389–393.

Tervoort, B. (1964). Development of language and "the critical period" in the young deaf child: Identification and management. *Acta Otolaryngologica, 206* (suppl.), 247–251.

Thoman, E. B. (1981). Affective communication as the prelude and context for language learning. In R. L. Schiefelbusch & D. D. Bricker (Eds.), *Early*

Language: Acquisition and Intervention (pp. 181–200). Baltimore: University Park Press.

Thompson, G., & Weber, B. A. (1974). Responses of infants and young children to behavior observation audiometry. *Journal of Speech and Hearing Disorders, 39,* 140–147.

Tiegerman, E., & Siperstein, M. (1984). Individual patterns of interaction in the mother-child dyad: Implications for parent intervention. *Topics in Language Disorders, 4,* 50–61.

Trehub, S. E., & Schneider, B. A. (1983). Recent advances in the behavioral study of infant audition. In S. E. Gerber & G. T. Mencher (Eds.), *The Development of Auditory Behavior* (pp. 167–185). New York: Grune and Stratton.

Trehub, S. E., Schneider, B. A., & Endman, M. (1980). Developmental changes in infants' sensitivity to octave-band noises. *Journal of Experimental Child Psychology, 29,* 282–293.

Trevarthen, C. (1977). Descriptive analyses of infant communicative behavior. In H. R. Schaffer (Ed.), *Studies on Mother-Infant Interaction* (pp. 227–270). London: Academic Press.

van Kleeck, A. (1985). Issues in adult-child interaction: Six philosophical orientations. *Topics in Language Disorders, 5,* 1–15.

Vaughn, P. (1981). *Learning to Listen: A Book by Mothers of Hearing-impaired Children.* Don Mills, Ontario: General Publishing Co.

Vihman, M. M. (1988a). Early phonological development. In J. E. Bernthal & N. W. Bankson (Eds.), *Articulation and Phonological Disorders* (2nd ed., pp. 60–109). Englewood Cliffs, NJ: Prentice Hall.

Vihman, M. M. (1988b). Later phonological development. In J. E. Bernthal & N. W. Bankson (Eds.), *Articulation and Phonological Disorders* (2nd ed., pp. 110–144). Englewood Cliffs, NJ: Prentice Hall.

Vihman, M. M., Ferguson, C. A., & Elbert, M. (1986). Phonological development from babbling to speech: Common tendencies and individual differences. *Applied Psycholinguistics, 7,* 3–40.

Vihman, M. M., & Greenlea, M. (1987). Individual differences in phonological development: Ages one and three years. *Journal of Speech and Hearing Disorders, 30,* 503–521.

Vygotsky, L. (1978). *Mind in Society.* Cambridge, MA: Harvard University Press.

Wanska, S. K., & Bedrosian, J. L. (1985). Conversational structure and topic performance in mother-child interaction. *Journal of Speech and Hearing Research, 28,* 579–584.

Webster, E. J., (1977). *Counseling with Parents of Handicapped Children: Guidelines for Improving Communication*. New York: Grune and Stratton.

Wedell-Monnig, J., & Lumley, J. M. (1980). Child deafness and mother-child interaction. *Child Development, 51*, 766–774.

Wedell-Monning, J., & Westerman, Y. B. (1977). *Mother's Language to Deaf and Hearing Infants*. Report No. FL-009-164 (ERIC Document Reproduction Service No. ED 149 595).

Whetnall, E. (1958). Clinics for children handicapped by deafness. In A. Ewing (Ed.), *The Modern Educational Treatment of Deafness* (pp. 16/1–16/11). Manchester, UK: Manchester University Press.

White, B. L. (1985). *The First Three Years of Life*. New York: Prentice Hall Press.

White, S. J., & White, R. E. C. (1984) The deaf imperative: Characteristics of maternal input to hearing-impaired children. *Topics in Language Disorders, 4*, 28–49.

Wilson, W. R., & Gerber, S. E. (1983). Auditory behavior in infancy. In S. E. Gerber & G. T. Mencher (Eds.), *The Development of Auditory Behavior* (pp. 149–166). New York: Grune and Stratton.

Winner, E. (1979). New names for old things: The emergence of metaphoric language. *Journal of Child Language, 6*, 469–491.

Wood, D. J. (1982). The linguistic experiences of the pre-lingually hearing-impaired child. *Journal of the British Association of Teachers of the Deaf, 6*, 86–93.

Yantis, P. A. (1985). Pure tone air condition testing. In J. Katz (Ed.), *Handbook of Clinical Audiology* (3rd ed.), (pp. 153–169). Baltimore, MD: Williams and Wilkins.

Zlatin, M. A., & Horii, Y. (1976). *Language Acquisition: Some Acoustic and Interactive Aspects of Infancy: Final Report*. NIE Grant NE-G-00-3-0077 (ERIC Document Reproduction Service No. ED 138141).

Index